Office of the
Comptroller of the Currency

Annual Report

Fiscal Year **2012**

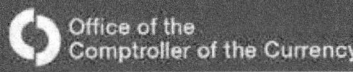

Office of the
Comptroller of the Currency

Publication No. AR-2012

OCC Locations

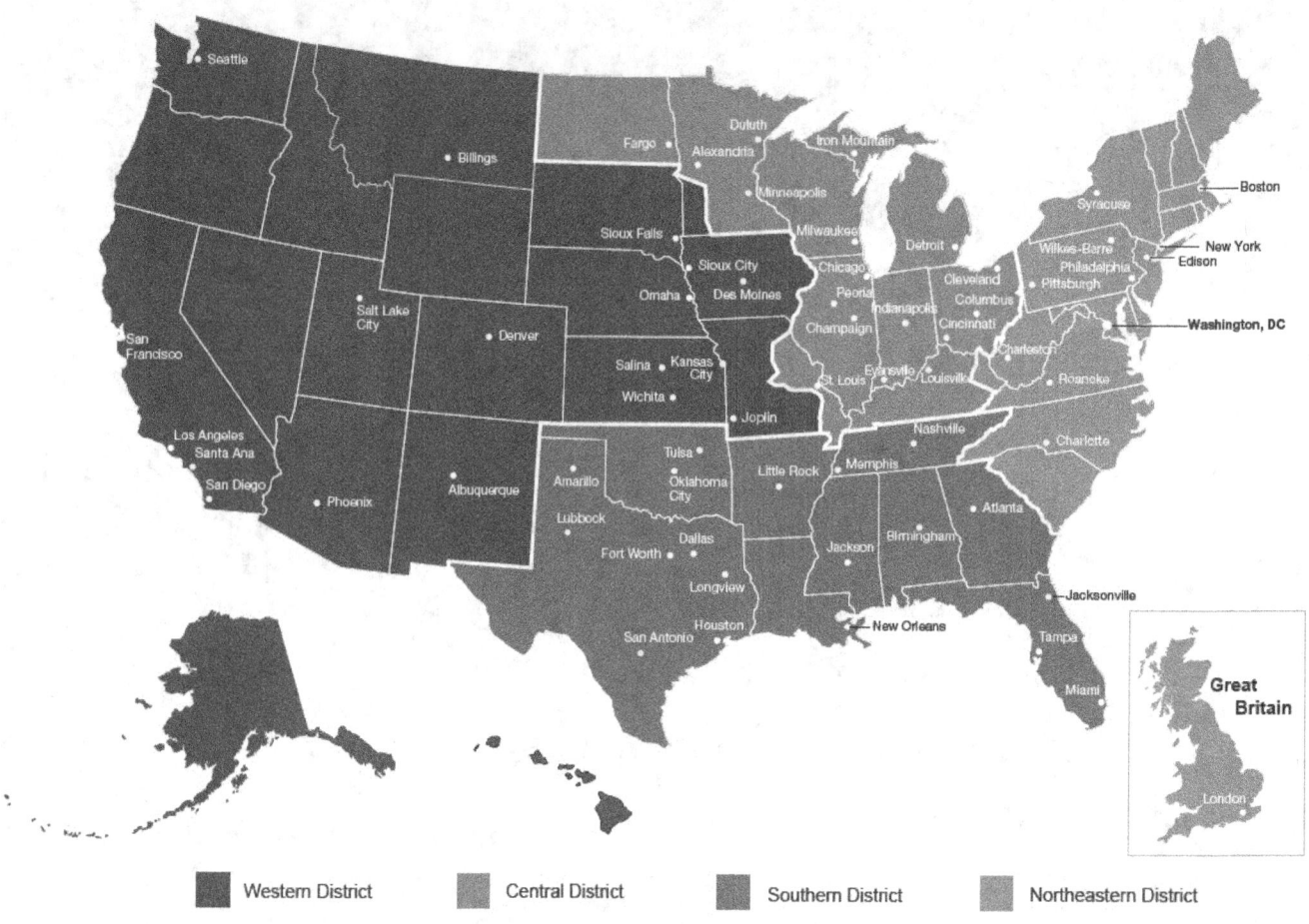

Western District   Central District   Southern District   Northeastern District

Federal Banking System at-a-Glance	
All OCC-supervised institutions, total assets	$10.1 trillion
All OCC-supervised institutions, share of total U.S. commercial banking assets	71 percent
All OCC-supervised institutions	1,971
Large banks	47
Midsize banks	47
Community banks	1,257
Federal branches	47
Federal savings associations	573

The OCC at-a-Glance	
Employees (full-time-equivalents)	3,823
Office locations*	66
Budget authority	$1.23 billion
Revenue derived from assessments	96.4 percent
Consumer complaints opened	66,161
Consumer complaints closed or referred	59,130

* The OCC maintains multiple locations in some large cities. In addition, the OCC has a continuous, on-site presence at large banks under its supervision.

About the OCC

The Office of the Comptroller of the Currency's (OCC) mission is to charter, regulate, and supervise national banks and federal savings associations[1] and to supervise the federal branches and agencies of foreign banks. The OCC's goal is to ensure that these institutions operate in a safe and sound manner and in compliance with laws requiring fair treatment of their customers and fair access to credit and financial products. The OCC is an independent bureau of the U.S. Department of the Treasury.

The President nominates the Comptroller of the Currency subject to confirmation by the U.S. Senate. The Comptroller also serves as a director of the Federal Deposit Insurance Corporation (FDIC) and NeighborWorks America.

Headquartered in Washington, D.C., the OCC has four district offices plus an office in London, which supervises the international activities of national banks. The OCC's nationwide staff of bank examiners conducts on-site reviews of banks and provides sustained supervision of these institutions' operations. Examiners analyze loan and investment portfolios, funds management, capital, earnings, liquidity, sensitivity to market risk for all banks, and compliance with consumer banking laws governing banks with $10 billion or less in assets. They also evaluate management's ability to identify and control risk.

In supervising banks, the OCC has the power to

- examine the banks.
- approve or deny applications for new charters, branches, capital, or other changes in corporate or banking structure.

- take supervisory and enforcement actions against banks that do not comply with laws and regulations or that otherwise engage in unsound practices.
- remove and prohibit officers and directors, negotiate agreements to change banking practices, and issue cease-and-desist orders as well as civil money penalties (CMP).
- issue rules and regulations, legal interpretations, and corporate decisions governing investments, lending, and other practices.

The OCC and the federal banking system were created by the National Currency Act, which President Abraham Lincoln signed into law on February 25, 1863. In June 1864, the law was substantially revised and expanded and given a new name: the National Bank Act. It remains the basic statute under which the OCC and the federal banking system operate today.

The first Comptroller of the Currency was Hugh McCulloch, formerly the president of the state-chartered Bank of Indiana. McCulloch went to Washington to argue against passage of the National

---

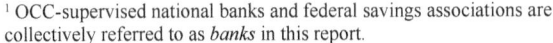

[1] OCC-supervised national banks and federal savings associations are collectively referred to as *banks* in this report.

About This Annual Report

Section 61 of the National Currency Act of February 25, 1863, directed the Comptroller of the Currency to "report annually to Congress … a summary of the state and condition" of the national banking system, along with suggestions for "any amendment to the laws relative to banking" or "other information in relation to [banking] associations as, in his judgment, may prove useful." Over the past century and a half, some of the most significant changes to the U.S. financial system—including the amendments to the National Currency Act enacted by Congress at the urging of Comptroller Hugh McCulloch as the National Bank Act of 1864—began with recommendations contained within the pages of this report. Since that time, the OCC *Annual Report* has chronicled and advanced the long evolution of the nation's financial and regulatory structure, providing the American people and their representatives with information vital to the country's economic security and well being.

Currency Act but soon came to appreciate its merits. Salmon P. Chase, Lincoln's Secretary of the Treasury, asked him to lead the new system, and McCulloch agreed.

Under McCulloch, his successors, and a professional staff of national bank examiners, the new system made an important contribution to the robust growth of the U.S. economy. National banks under OCC supervision issued a uniform national currency, which replaced the previous varied and unreliable money supply, and provided financial services across the country.

The National Bank Act endows the OCC with considerable operational independence. The OCC does not receive appropriations from Congress. Instead, the OCC's operations are funded primarily through assessments on the financial institutions it supervises.

On July 21, 2011, under provisions of the Dodd–Frank Wall Street Reform and Consumer Protection Act of 2010,[2] the Office of Thrift Supervision (OTS) became part of the OCC. As a result, the OCC is responsible for the supervision of federal savings associations, under the Home Owners' Loan Act.

---

[2] Hereafter referred to as *Dodd–Frank* in this report.

Contents

Comptroller's Viewpoint

As I write this introduction to the OCC's fiscal year (FY) 2012 *Annual Report,* it is a little more than six months since the Senate confirmed my nomination as the 30th Comptroller of the Currency. For a career bank supervisor like myself, there is no higher honor than to assume a place among the distinguished Americans who have built and burnished the OCC's reputation for excellence.

Since I arrived at the OCC in April 2012, three key anniversaries have come and gone. It has been five years since the start of the worst financial crisis since the Great Depression, two years since the Dodd–Frank Wall Street Reform and Consumer Protection Act altered the financial regulatory landscape, and one year since the integration of the Office of Thrift Supervision into the OCC. And next year will bring a fourth milestone that is very important to those of us at the OCC: the 150th anniversary of the passage of the National Currency Act of 1863, which created the federal banking system and the OCC as its supervisor. In its own way, each of these events influences my agenda as Comptroller.

The financial crisis was a powerful reminder that a safe and sound banking system is indispensable to our nation's economic health. That's why, at my Senate confirmation hearings, I publicly committed myself to the cause of robust supervision. I further promised that we would continually reexamine our own supervisory policies and procedures and take all necessary steps to enhance them.

Specifically, strong supervision means setting high standards and holding the national banks and federal savings associations we supervise (and ourselves) to those standards. It means making sure that banks have appropriate processes, procedures, and contingency plans to address the full spectrum of risk applicable to those institutions. It also demands that the OCC establish clear and reasonable rules and that our procedures enforce those rules consistently and fairly.

As someone who has been involved in bank supervision for more than 25 years, I have learned how important it is that supervision be fair and reasonable. The institutions we oversee play a vital role in supporting strong communities and economic growth by serving the financial needs of individuals, communities, and businesses, and we don't want to hamstring those efforts with supervision that is overly burdensome, arbitrary, or unpredictable. At the same time, it is important that the industry and the public recognize that supervisors take strong action—including public enforcement actions requiring payment of CMPs and restitution— to correct problems.

Several initiatives to enhance OCC supervision were under way when I became Comptroller, and those initiatives continue. U.S. bank supervisors are working together to raise capital standards because the financial crisis demonstrated yet again that a safe and sound banking system requires capital of sufficient quantity and quality to meet all reasonable contingencies. It is a measure of the industry's growing health that capital, both in absolute terms and in relation to the risks embedded in bank loan portfolios, is stronger today than it has been in many years. Progress has also been made in bolstering liquidity, addressing a weakness that was exposed during the period of low market confidence in 2008–2009. We've raised supervisory standards for risk management, including the management of operational risk, which has been a matter of particular concern of late.

We set heightened expectations for corporate oversight and governance at our largest banks. For example, while supervisors long operated on the premise that oversight functions rated as "satisfactory" were sufficient, we now require large banks to achieve a rating of "strong" in their audit and risk management functions. We expect members of each bank's board and its executive management team to ensure that audit and risk management receive visible and substantive support. Our examiners evaluate the transition from "satisfactory" to "strong" in these two key oversight functions as part of their ongoing supervision. When we find weaknesses, we require corrective action.

We see considerable evidence that our heightened expectations for corporate oversight and governance are taking hold—that the people and systems behind our largest banks are better prepared to meet the challenge of running these complex and powerful financial institutions.

But we cannot afford to be complacent—certainly not at a time when the banking system and the U.S. economy are facing strong headwinds at home and abroad.

Community banks face special challenges. Some of the communities they serve have yet to participate in the economic recovery. Community banks tend to hold concentrations of residential and commercial real estate loans—two products that performed especially poorly during the recession. Not only have these banks had to write off disproportionate numbers of bad loans, but they also have had trouble finding creditworthy borrowers in this difficult economic environment. This situation has pressured bank profitability. Community banks also face new regulatory requirements. These circumstances explain why some question the future of the community bank franchise and why some veteran community bankers have decided to leave the business.

The OCC is committed to ensuring that community banking remains safe and sound. We devote the bulk of our resources to community bank supervision. We work closely with the banks we supervise to help them identify their strengths, correct their weaknesses, and build their businesses in a safe and sound manner. Our community bank supervision is carried out by examiners who are knowledgeable, experienced, and sensitive to the circumstances under which their institutions operate. Our supervision program combines the perspective of local examiners with the perspective of a national organization.

Regulatory burden seems always to fall most heavily on those institutions that are least equipped to handle it—namely, banks that don't have a deep bench of consultants and lawyers to help steer them through the thickets. Thus, one of the most important contributions we can make—especially at a time of regulatory change—is to help minimize that burden. We are doing this by making sure we apply the rules with a view to the unique challenges facing community banks. As discussed in this *Annual Report,* we have done just that in a number of the Dodd–Frank rulemakings relating to stress testing and credit ratings, for example.

To address that challenge as effectively as possible, it is important for us to listen to the men and women who lead community banks. We have an ambitious outreach program that takes me and other OCC senior managers around the country to speak with—and listen to—community bankers. I look forward to continuing this dialogue in the coming months and years.

Last year's *Annual Report* observed that Dodd–Frank implementation and international efforts to strengthen capital standards were the OCC's major preoccupations in FY 2011. That was still true in FY 2012. Though many key rulemakings were finalized in 2012, as detailed in this *Annual Report,* others are still developing. Proposed revisions to the risk-based capital rules, the risk retention rule for asset securitizations, and the Volcker rule on proprietary trading generated enormous interest from the financial industry and other concerned parties. While the OCC intends to move forward with these rulemakings in an expeditious manner, it is also important to consider all the ramifications of these proposed rules.

The integration of the bulk of the people and supervisory functions of the OTS into the OCC, as mandated by Dodd–Frank, is continuing on schedule. The success of this massive undertaking is a matter of particular pride to me and should be to everyone who had a hand in making it happen.

The OCC's 150th anniversary in February 2013 will be more than a celebration of the vision of our founders, especially President Abraham Lincoln, Secretary of the Treasury Salmon P. Chase, and the first Comptroller, Hugh McCulloch. We will also celebrate the values that have distinguished the OCC since its creation: professionalism, independence, and a commitment to a strong, integrated national economy. In my career as a bank supervisor, I have experienced the savings and loan and bank crises of the late 1980s and early 1990s, as well as the more recent financial crisis that shook the U.S. and global economies. We have learned that risks to the banking system can come from many directions, and it is our job to be alert to them all. This is a challenge the OCC has met throughout its 150-year history and one I am confident we will continue to meet in the years to come. I welcome the opportunity to lead this vital organization into the future.

Thomas J. Curry
Comptroller of the Currency

Section One
Year in Review

Introduction

On April 9, 2012, Thomas J. Curry became the 30th Comptroller of the Currency, assuming the leadership of an agency dedicated to the oversight of federally chartered financial institutions. Today, the OCC is an organization of bank examiners, attorneys, economists, and other professionals working together to accomplish its vital mission in the best interests of citizens, banks, and the nation's economy.

Testifying before the U.S. Senate Committee on Banking, Housing, and Urban Affairs for the first time after his confirmation, Comptroller Curry reaffirmed the OCC's commitment to "strong, effective supervision."[3] To that end, the OCC in FY 2012[4] focused its efforts on assessing and enhancing the ability of the banks it supervises to identify, measure, monitor, and control risk.

During the year, the agency supplemented and updated its comprehensive guidance to bankers and examiners, helping them respond to emerging risks. It reviewed and revised procedures to ensure that banks operate in full compliance with fair lending, consumer protection, information security, and Bank Secrecy Act/Anti-Money Laundering (BSA/AML) requirements. It continued to root out and require correction of unsafe and unsound practices in the origination and servicing of mortgage loans. It monitored and analyzed the health of the economy and the banking system,

Comptroller Thomas J. Curry testifies on OCC supervision before a congressional committee. Paul Nash, Senior Deputy Comptroller and Chief of Staff, is at right.

disseminating that information through an extensive program of publications and outreach. Finally, the OCC worked alongside other federal agencies to implement Dodd–Frank and other regulatory initiatives to create stronger, more resilient financial institutions, more transparent financial markets, more robust consumer protections, and more effective instruments to deal with troubled or insolvent banks.

Supervisory Initiatives

The OCC's mission has always been to ensure that the financial institutions under its supervision are both safe and sound. Safe banks operate within all legal and regulatory boundaries and protect the interests of depositors, shareholders, employees, and the citizens who depend on them and stand behind them. Sound

---

[3] Statement of Thomas J. Curry, Comptroller of the Currency, Committee on Banking, Housing, and Urban Affairs, U.S. Senate, June 6, 2012, www.occ.gov. All citations in this report's footnotes that refer to the OCC Web site can be found on the About the OCC, News and Issuances, or Publications pages.

[4] Unless otherwise noted, all references to 2012 refer to the fiscal year beginning October 1, 2011, and ending September 30, 2012.

banks operate as responsible businesses, earning returns sufficient to attract investment, competent management, and customer support.

Once viewed as an intermittent process that began when the agency's examiners arrived at a bank and ended when they departed, bank supervision is now a continuous and comprehensive process scaled to the size, condition, and complexity of each institution. The OCC assesses banks' conditions and risk-management capabilities, performs ongoing assessments of the health of the market or markets within which banks operate, develops and refines regulations and guidance based on the requirements of law and the conditions in the industry, and regulates the industry's operational and competitive structure through the agency's licensing activities.

The information gathered from the supervisory activity at each bank enables the agency's four districts and its Washington, D.C., headquarters to monitor the system's overall safety and soundness, focusing operational and policy responses on those banks, banking activities, and financial markets that pose the most significant challenges. The OCC calls this system *risk-based supervision,* and it defines the agency's approach to its mission.

The OCC's Supervisory Programs

The OCC's midsize and community bank supervision program is built around a network of local field offices in more than 60 cities throughout the United States. Each bank is assigned to an examiner who continuously monitors the bank's condition and serves as the focal point for communications between the OCC and the bank. This approach ensures that midsize and community banks receive the benefits of highly trained examiners with local knowledge and experience, along with the resources and specialized expertise provided by a nationwide organization. Using a common framework and set of expectations, examiners tailor their supervision of each bank to its individual risk profile, business model, and management strategies.

The OCC's large bank supervision program is headquartered in Washington, D.C., providing a national perspective that facilitates coordination across large institutions. It is based on a continuous, on-site presence at each of the United States' 19 largest banking companies. At each large bank, an Examiner-in-Charge manages a staff of some of the OCC's most seasoned examiners. They are supported by economists, legal staff, and various policy and subject matter specialists.

On-site examination teams study the objectives of the bank and its lines of business, the key risks it faces, and the controls that are put in place to manage them. Examiners assess the levels of risk in the bank and the quality of risk management over the course of the examination cycle. Finally, examiners are charged with communicating examination findings, concerns, and ratings. The examiners also ensure that corrective actions are taken through the supervisory process or through appropriate enforcement actions. OCC supervisory staff will continue to focus on the achievement of five heightened expectations for the 19 large banks:

- Board willingness to provide a credible challenge to management decisions
- Talent management and compensation processes
- Defining and communicating risk appetite across the company
- Development and maintenance of strong audit and risk management functions
- Board responsibility to preserve the sanctity of the national bank charter

Assessing Risk

Banking is essentially the business of risk management. A bank's success depends on its ability to navigate the multiple risks inherent in the banking business.

Banks must contend with credit risk—the possibility that borrowers will fail to repay in accordance with the terms of their loan agreements. They deal with interest rate risk (IRR), which requires them to manage disparities between what they pay for funds and what their customers pay for the use of funds. Banks face liquidity risk to the extent that they are able or unable to meet their immediate financial obligations to customers and counterparties. Compliance risk relates to the damage that can result from failure to heed the laws and regulations that banks must follow. Reputation risk arises when a bank offers products or services that involve practices that deviate from the bank's standards, and it increases with poor service, inappropriate sales recommendations, or violations of consumer law, any of which may result in litigation, adverse publicity, and loss of business.

Market risk refers to the risk inherent in banks' trading activities. Strategic risk flows from changes in regulatory mandates, economic conditions, the competitive environment, and customer behavior that challenge banks' business models. Price risk involves the rise and fall in value of the securities in a bank's portfolio in response to market trends. Finally, operational risk refers to the perennial hazard that the systems, manual or electronic, that banks depend on may prove faulty or inadequate or that employees may fail to perform assigned duties or follow proper procedures.

Banks experience these risks in varying degrees, reflecting each bank's unique attributes of culture, market, processes, risk tolerance, and products and services. Effective bank supervision, therefore, requires a customized evaluation of the unique combinations of risk to which a bank is exposed and a supervisory approach tailored to the bank's particular circumstances and risk profile.

Depending on the nature and severity of the supervisory problems that they encounter, OCC examiners may resort to a range of supervisory

remedies that include designation of a "matter requiring attention" by the bank, restrictions on future activity, CMPs, removal from office of bank employees, or revocation of a bank's charter.[5]

At the conclusion of every community bank examination, the Examiner-in-Charge conducts a meeting with the board of directors to discuss the examination findings and OCC expectations.[6] This information provides bankers and directors with feedback about a bank's condition and the quality of its management. The OCC also relies on its examination reports to form a coherent picture of risk trends throughout the financial system, which in turn helps shape the agency's supervisory policies.

The OCC's National Risk Committee (NRC) monitors the condition of the banking system and emerging threats to the system's safety and soundness on an ongoing basis. The NRC communicates risk issues, coordinates with other supervisory and policy risk groups throughout the OCC, and develops policy recommendations. Its members are drawn from a broad spectrum of OCC specializations in bank supervision, economics, law, and policy, and its findings shape the OCC's supervisory policies and the guidance that implements those policies.

---

[5] "Bank Supervision Process," *Comptroller's Handbook*, www.occ.gov.

[6] OCC examiners of large and midsize banks provide regular feedback to bankers and boards of directors.

In 2012 for the first time, the NRC published its findings in the *Semiannual Risk Perspective*, a report that evaluates threats to bank safety and soundness.[7] This report examines the operating environment for banks, looks at their earnings and performance, and addresses key risk factors, including trends in credit, funding, liquidity, and interest rate exposures, and the regulatory climate.

The spring 2012 report focused on three major risk concerns: the aftereffects of the recent housing-driven credit boom-bust cycle; the challenges to banking industry revenue growth in a post-recession, slow-growth economy; and the potential that banks may take excessive risks in an effort to improve profitability.

The report found that large banks with extensive mortgage operations continued to be challenged by the remediation costs, record penalties, and reputational damage caused by previous conduct and by the continuing backlog of severely delinquent and in-process-of-foreclosure mortgages.

Asset-quality indicators showed improvement across small and large banks, although housing-related loans continued to experience above-average rates of delinquency and charge-off. Commercial real estate performance improved, but vacancy rates and the level of problem assets remained high—a particular concern for many community lenders.

Many of the challenges facing bankers stemmed from the slow recovery of the national and global economy, the report found. Persistent unemployment and

cautious consumers have crimped loan demand and suppressed bank income. The report raises the possibility that earnings pressures, higher regulatory costs, and reduced fee income could prompt banks to take on additional credit risk and cut back on essential systems and processes, which would increase operational risk.

Managing Credit Risk

The OCC views credit risk as "the primary financial risk in the banking system. ... [It] exists in virtually all income-producing activities. How a bank selects and manages its credit risk is critically important to its performance over time; indeed, capital depletion through loan losses has been the proximate cause of most institution failures."[8] The amount of credit risk embedded in its balance sheet and how well that risk is controlled are thus critical determinants of a bank's overall safety and soundness.

Banks employ different strategies to control credit risk. They may make fewer loans or become more selective or restrictive about the loans they do make. They may limit their exposure to less creditworthy borrowers and to particular economic and geographic segments in order to reduce the risk associated with excessive asset concentrations. They may tighten loan structures and impose more restrictive covenants, requiring additional or higher-quality collateral, and set more rigorous conditions on how and when borrowers may draw upon funds. They may also bolster capital and reserves against loan losses.

The OCC monitors credit risk at the management level, where institutions determine their tolerance for risk and establish the policies that govern extensions of credit, and at the operational level, where loans are evaluated under bank-approved guidelines. The structure and pricing of the loan products that emerge from bank credit analysis reflect the operational integrity and direction of credit risk in the bank.

For 18 years, the OCC has been polling its examiners about credit underwriting practices in the banks they supervise and publishing the results as the *Survey of Credit Underwriting Practices*.[9] In 2012, the survey

---

[7] *Semiannual Risk Perspective*, spring 2012, www.occ.gov.

[8] "Rating Credit Risk," *Comptroller's Handbook*, www.occ.gov.

[9] *2012 Survey of Credit Underwriting Practices*, www.occ.gov.

incorporated responses from examiners at 87 banks with $3 billion or more in assets, totaling $4.6 trillion, or 91 percent of all loans in the federal banking system. The study covered 11 commercial and seven retail loan products.

Seventy percent of examiners reported no change in underwriting standards for commercial loans since the previous survey. Some easing of underwriting standards, however, was noted within certain commercial and retail products, including indirect consumer loans, credit cards, large corporate, asset-based lending, and leveraged loans. Easing generally took the form of lower pricing, lower credit score cut-offs, and reduced collateral requirements. Examiners found that lenders that eased underwriting standards typically were motivated by a perception that the economic outlook had improved, by a modest increase in competition for the same loans, by a desire for growth, and by increased market liquidity. Over the next 12 months, examiners believe, credit risk will

likely increase for 25 percent of the loan products, decrease for 24 percent, and remain unchanged for 51 percent. Similar to the 2011 survey results, the 2012 survey indicated that the majority of banks generally apply the same underwriting standards to loans underwritten with the intent to hold as to those underwritten with the intent to sell.

The survey's finding that underwriting standards for leveraged-lending products had eased highlighted one area of particular regulatory concern in 2012. *Leveraged lending* is a term broadly used to describe a type of corporate finance used for mergers and acquisitions, business recapitalization and refinancing, equity buyouts, and business or product line build-outs and expansions. In these transactions, debt is commonly used as an alternative to equity for financing business expansions and acquisitions. Properly used, leveraged loans can support business growth and increase shareholder returns.[10]

Only 15 percent of banks covered in the survey were reported to have engaged in leveraged lending, and they were almost exclusively large and midsize banks. But what stood out in 2012—as it did in 2011—was the pronounced trend toward easing underwriting standards in that product segment. Thirty-eight percent of the leveraged lenders covered in the survey eased underwriting; none tightened. Moreover, leveraged-loan volumes, which had dropped off sharply during the financial crisis, rebounded strongly, magnifying the potential impact of the softer standards used to underwrite these loans.

Responding to this trend in its early stages, the OCC participated in the formulation of proposed revised interagency guidance that seeks to focus lenders' attention on the specific risk-management challenges associated with leveraged lending. The guidance assigned explicit responsibility to bank managers and boards of directors for establishing thresholds for risk, for developing effective control systems, and for acting decisively when an institution's established threshold for risk is exceeded. The guidance also outlined the banking agencies' expectations for leveraged-lending underwriting standards, emphasizing "that the business premise for each transaction should be sound and its

---

[10] "Leveraged Lending," *Comptroller's Handbook*, www.occ.gov.

capital structure should be sustainable, irrespective of whether underwritten to hold [in the bank's loan portfolio] or distribute."[11] The comment period for the revised leveraged-lending guidance closed in June; the final guidance was expected to be released in the fall of 2012.

In 2012, several broad measures of overall credit risk among banks showed signs of improvement. Asset quality improved; delinquency and charge-off rates fell; and banks were able to lower provisions for loan losses, increasing the resources available for their own and their customers' use.

Yet, as noted above, banks face risk from many sources that could affect the collectability of loans. The OCC carefully monitored bank reserves throughout the year to ensure that they were adequate to cover probable loan losses.

Banks in parts of the country that had yet to participate in the national economic recovery continued to contend with higher levels of problem loans. Certain loan products, including commercial real estate, residential real estate, and home equity loans, continued to underperform other types of loans nationwide.

The weakness in those loan categories has been especially challenging for the community banks that compose the overwhelming majority of OCC-supervised institutions. Community banks provide essential support for the small businesses that play an important role in national economic development and

job creation.[12] The OCC's approach to community bank supervision recognizes that these institutions face credit risk management challenges that are very different from those facing larger, more-diversified financial companies.

Community banks are especially susceptible to concentration risk. The OCC defines an asset concentration as a pool of loan exposures "whose collective performance has the potential to affect a bank negatively even if each individual transaction within a pool is soundly underwritten."[13] Smaller banks are inherently more sensitive to the performance of the smaller number of individual credits they hold. Indeed, poorly managed asset concentrations, primarily in acquisition, development, and construction of commercial real estate, have been responsible for the majority of community bank failures over the past three years.

In a speech before the CRE Finance Council, Comptroller Curry acknowledged that concentrations are "a fact of life." He urged community banks to carefully manage their concentration risk by working with troubled borrowers to get and keep them current through hard times, monitoring concentration exposures, maintaining appropriate loan-loss reserves, and taking appropriate charge-offs when repayment becomes unlikely.[14]

To guide examiners in helping banks manage concentration risk, the OCC issued a revised "Concentrations of Credit" booklet of the *Comptroller's Handbook*.[15] The new publication provides an enhanced definition of a credit concentration to encourage consideration of more than just the dollar amount of exposure and places renewed emphasis on stress testing—the use of models that project financial institution performance in various economic scenarios—to identify and quantify credit concentration risks.

---

[11] Office of the Comptroller of the Currency, "Request for Comment on Revised Leveraged Lending Guidance," bulletin 2012-9, March 30, 2012, www.occ.gov.

[12] For more on OCC programs to encourage lending to small business, see the *Annual Report FY 2011*, 26–27, www.occ.gov.

[13] "Concentrations of Credit," *Comptroller's Handbook*, www.occ.gov. See also Office of the Comptroller of the Currency, "Concentrations of Credit: Revised Booklet," bulletin 2011-48, December 13, 2011, www.occ.gov.

[14] Remarks by Thomas J. Curry, CRE Finance Council, June 13, 2012, www.occ.gov.

[15] "Concentrations of Credit," *Comptroller's Handbook*, www.occ.gov. See also Office of the Comptroller of the Currency, "Concentrations of Credit: Revised Booklet," bulletin 2011-48, December 13, 2011, www.occ.gov.

Comptroller Curry discusses the condition of the U.S. banking system and operational risk at an economic and financial forum in Washington, D.C.

Managing Interest Rate Risk

Some degree of IRR is inherent in the business of banking. Banks are expected to have sound risk management practices in place to measure, monitor, and control IRR exposures. In the current low interest-rate environment, many banks have experienced a surge in deposit growth, which makes it particularly important that bankers reassess their IRR modeling assumptions.

In January 2012, the financial regulators issued Frequently Asked Questions (FAQ) on the 2010 interagency advisory on IRR management.[16] This document addresses critical risk management practices including robust and meaningful stress testing, assumption development that reflects the institution's experience, and comprehensive model validation. This

discussion was especially timely for small federal savings associations in their efforts to implement an independent IRR measurement process for earnings and capital at risk following the migration from the former OTS's IRR model at the end of 2011. The OCC conducted outreach to federal savings associations focused on the OCC's IRR management expectations.

Managing Liquidity Risk

Bankers were once able to rely on a core of stable, low-cost consumer deposits to fund their loans and investments. But deregulation and the end of interest rate ceilings required bankers to look beyond their retail deposit base to wholesale sources of funding, such as brokered deposits, repurchase agreements, and correspondent-bank and federal-funds lines of credit. Managing the mix of retail deposits and wholesale funding to meet expected liquidity needs has become a critical challenge for bankers.

In 2012 the OCC issued a revised "Liquidity" booklet in the *Comptroller's Handbook* providing supplementary guidance to examiners and bankers on assessing the quantity of liquidity risk exposure and the quality of liquidity risk management. It placed new emphasis on the importance of maintaining appropriate levels of highly liquid assets and planning for contingency funding in case wholesale liquidity becomes unavailable.[17]

Managing Operational Risk

It was "an extraordinary thing," Comptroller Curry said in a May speech. "Some of our most seasoned supervisors, people with 30 or more years of experience in some cases, tell me that this is the first time they have seen operational risk eclipse credit risk as a safety and soundness challenge."[18] In 2012, operational risk and the consequences of operational risk management failure manifested themselves in many forms.[19]

---

[16] Office of the Comptroller of the Currency, "FAQs on 2010 Interagency Advisory on Interest Rate Risk Management," bulletin 2012-5, January 12, 2012, www.occ.gov.

[17] "Liquidity," *Comptroller's Handbook,* www.occ.gov.

[18] Remarks by Thomas J. Curry, Exchequer Club, May 16, 2012, www.occ.gov.

[19] A complete list of OCC enforcement actions is on page 33.

Implementing the Mortgage Foreclosure Agreement

In April 2011, the OCC and other federal banking agencies imposed sweeping enforcement actions against 14 large mortgage servicers for having engaged in unsafe and unsound mortgage servicing and foreclosure practices in 2009 and 2010. The consent orders require the companies to hire independent consultants who, under the regulators' supervision, identify borrowers injured financially as a direct result of errors that occurred during the foreclosure process and provide those borrowers with one or more forms of remediation. The order also requires the companies to improve their servicing and foreclosure practices to protect future borrowers from such injury. The actions sought to fulfill the OCC's commitment to "fix what was broken; identify borrowers who were financially harmed; provide compensation for that injury; and, make sure this doesn't happen again."[20]

When an injured borrower is identified—either through the borrower's request for review or as the result of a file review conducted by the independent consultants—the borrower may receive remediation that could consist of a lump-sum payment, a suspension or rescission of a foreclosure, a loan modification or other loss mitigation assistance, correction of credit reports, or correction of deficiency amounts and records. Under the orders, there are no limits to the overall amount of compensation that can be paid out or the remediation action offered.

As stipulated in the engagement letters that defined their responsibilities, the independent consultants are reviewing a base sample of more than 142,000 loan files from the servicers' portfolios. That includes every loan in certain categories of foreclosure cases—for example, borrowers subject to the Servicemembers Civil Relief Act (SCRA). The independent consultants are expected to review additional loans as the process continues and as patterns that require additional investigation come to light.

Beginning in November 2011, the OCC and the servicers' independent consultants launched an extensive campaign to inform eligible borrowers of the opportunity to request a review, free of charge, if they believed they had been harmed by the practices of mortgage servicers subject to the consent order. Nearly 4.4 million letters were sent to borrowers who had been in the process of foreclosure in 2009 or 2010. Additional follow-up mailings were sent to borrowers who did not respond. A Web site, https://independentforeclosurereview.com, and a toll-free telephone number were created to provide information and answer questions about the claims process. Paid advertising ran in more than a thousand publications and on radio stations nationwide; public service announcements ran in print and broadcast media; servicers funded direct outreach through a variety of community groups; and the OCC and the Federal Reserve held training conferences for community and housing advocates and Web seminars to help educate housing counselors and increase awareness of the foreclosure review process.[21]

To promote the broadest participation possible, the two agencies extended the deadline for submitting requests for independent review to December 31, 2012.[22]

While the enforcement action provides remedies for injuries suffered in the past, it also contains provisions designed to improve mortgage-servicing processes going forward. The order requires servicers

---

[20] Statement of Morris Morgan, Deputy Comptroller for Large Bank Supervision, Committee on Oversight and Government Reform, U.S. House of Representatives, March 19, 2012, www.occ.gov.

[21] Office of the Comptroller of the Currency, "Interim Status Report: Foreclosure-Related Consent Orders," June 2012, www.occ.gov. This publication updates the previous interim report published in November 2011.

[22] Office of the Comptroller of the Currency, "Deadline to Request Independent Foreclosure Review Extended to December 31," news release 2012-117, August 2, 2012, www.occ.gov.

to implement 97 separate corrective measures to address specified unsafe and unsound practices. Those measures fall into several broad categories: developing comprehensive action plans; building strong compliance mechanisms; enhancing third-party management; upgrading management information systems; and reforming the Mortgage Electronic Registration System, which tracks changes in mortgage servicing rights and ownership interests. Although national mortgage servicers have reported significant progress in accomplishing these corrective measures, the OCC is continuing to monitor, validate, and, as necessary, require the correction of work under way to implement servicers' action plans.

Bank Secrecy Act and Anti-Money Laundering Compliance

Since it was enacted in 1970, the BSA has required banks to maintain records and file reports that were of use to law enforcement and regulators in combating money laundering and other financial crimes. In the last four decades, BSA/AML regulatory requirements and supervisory expectations have increased significantly, requiring institutions to make substantial improvements in their BSA/AML compliance programs. Many institutions have invested in suspicious activity monitoring systems to assist in identifying suspicious activity related to money laundering and terrorist financing. These systems also are used to report suspicious activity

Initiatives to Promote Financing for Permanent Housing

As a matter of both good business and public responsibility, banks are active supporters of projects that enhance the well-being of the communities they serve. For its part, the OCC disseminates industry best practices, promotes public-private collaboration, and informs the institutions it supervises of the obligations and opportunities available under the Community Reinvestment Act and other legislation.

One OCC initiative in 2012 focused on ways that banks can help to address the plight of the men, women, and children who lack permanent homes. Although the percentage of the population defined as homeless has declined over the last decade, the problem remains acute.

Studies show that one of the best ways to move toward the national goal of ending chronic homelessness by 2015 is to provide permanent supportive housing (PSH)—an approach that combines affordable rental housing with services to help tenants remain in their homes and avoid becoming homeless again. The OCC's February 2012 *Community Developments Investments* newsletter described the innovative strategies being employed by banks to support communities that have developed PSH plans. Some of these strategies take advantage of the Low-Income Housing Tax Credit and New Markets Tax Credit programs to invest in equity funds that not only build and manage housing projects but also provide a range of services to their residents, including mental health counseling, substance abuse treatment, educational programs, and job training. In other cases, banks invest directly in PSH projects through their own community development departments or aid the effort by transferring foreclosed multifamily properties to developers for renovation. Banks also make cash grants and contributions of their employees' time and expertise to nonprofit organizations that help people who are homeless. Efforts like these may receive positive consideration under the Community Reinvestment Act.[23]

---

[23] Office of the Comptroller of the Currency, *Community Developments Investments*, "Ending Homelessness: Financing Permanent Supportive Housing," February 2012, www.occ.gov.

OCC employees provide information to participants on Financial Literacy Day on Capitol Hill.

- increased the resources and expertise devoted to BSA/AML supervision;
- improved examiner training on emerging threats and vulnerabilities;
- kept the financial services industry abreast of OCC expectations;
- developed enhanced risk identification and analysis tools for the industry's use;
- stepped up formal coordination with other concerned federal agencies;
- refined its testing and sampling techniques to ensure that banks effectively identify suspicious transactions; and
- brought strong enforcement actions against banks found to be in non-compliance with BSA/AML requirements.

In the past 10 years, the OCC has issued more than 180 formal enforcement actions based in whole or in part on BSA/AML violations, including 24 during 2012.

In April 2012, for example, the OCC issued a consent cease-and-desist order against one large national bank for violations of the BSA and underlying regulations. The OCC found that the bank's BSA compliance program had deficiencies with respect to internal controls, customer due diligence, independent BSA auditing function, monitoring of remote deposit capture and international cash letter instrument processing, and suspicious activity reporting. The order required the bank to take comprehensive corrective actions to ensure the independence of the bank's compliance staff, to automate and make accessible all customer due diligence processes, and to conduct a review of its remote deposit capture activity.[24]

The OCC's supervision and enforcement actions with respect to HSBC Bank USA were the focus of a July 2012 report by the Senate Committee on Homeland Security and Governmental Affairs' Permanent Subcommittee on Investigations. The report criticized the OCC for not taking action soon enough and made

to law enforcement agencies and to ensure that such transactions do not involve entities subject to Office of Foreign Asset Control sanctions.

The individuals whose behavior the BSA was enacted to stop, however, also have become more determined and sophisticated. Today, the challenge comes not only from drug cartels and criminal organizations seeking to launder money through the U.S. financial system but also from terrorists and rogue regimes.

BSA and money-laundering problems have been on the rise throughout the financial system, and the OCC has worked hard to stay ahead of the growing challenge presented by BSA compliance. In the last year, the agency has

- updated and enhanced its BSA/AML examination procedures;

---

[24] Office of the Comptroller of the Currency, "OCC Issues Cease and Desist Order Against Citibank, N.A.," news release 2012-57, April 5, 2012, www.occ.gov.

specific recommendations to the OCC to improve its BSA/AML supervision, all of which are being implemented.

The OCC published a supervisory memorandum clarifying the composition and function of its Large Bank Review Team, which contributes independent perspective to the supervisory process to promote and ensure consistency in BSA/AML compliance and enforcement in large banks. The OCC also refined its approach to reporting BSA/AML violations in its examination reports and reaffirmed that because of the serious risk that such violations pose, examiners generally will downgrade the management component of the bank's rating under the Uniform Financial Institutions Rating System when serious BSA/AML deficiencies are identified.

Consumer Compliance

Dodd–Frank enacted substantial changes in the regulation of consumer financial services. The law endowed the new Consumer Financial Protection Bureau (CFPB) with important responsibilities for rulemaking across the financial system and for enforcement and supervision of certain consumer laws at banks with more than $10 billion in assets and previously unregulated non-banks.

Ensuring fair access and treatment of bank customers remains a fundamental part of the OCC's mission. OCC examiners continue to evaluate compliance with the Community Reinvestment Act (CRA) and flood insurance rules in banks of all sizes, as well as all consumer protection issues in banks with $10 billion or less in assets. The agency takes comprehensive enforcement actions when necessary to protect consumers' rights.

The partial transfer of consumer compliance responsibilities to the CFPB underscored the importance of coordination and collaboration between the CFPB and the federal banking agencies. In 2012, the OCC, along with the Board of Governors of the Federal Reserve System, the FDIC, and the National Credit Union Administration, agreed to a Memorandum of Understanding with the CFPB to coordinate key aspects of the supervision of banks with more than $10 billion in assets, to avoid unnecessary supervisory regulatory burden and

Cultivating OCC Skills and Leadership

The increased complexity of the financial regulatory system—and the steady retirement from the workplace of experienced OCC employees—make it imperative that the OCC identify, train, and nurture the next generation of professionals, who will inherit responsibility for the financial system's supervision. The OCC has a number of initiatives under way to ensure that the agency is building the specialized skills it needs to fulfill its important mission—not just next month or next year, but for decades to come.

One example is the EXCEL program, which was launched in 2012 and is based in the OCC's Large Bank Supervision Department. EXCEL recruits mid-level examiners committed to advancing their expertise in one of seven specialty areas: asset management, bank information technology, capital markets, commercial credit, compliance, operational risk, and retail credit. Successful candidates spend 12 to 24 months as part of a training team led by a senior OCC examiner, receiving formal instruction in the selected specialty area and participating in specialized examinations of OCC large banks. This accelerated development provides some of the OCC's most talented but less-experienced examiners with an important career-enhancing experience and the agency with a cadre of high-level specialists ready to step into leadership roles in the future.

overlap. The agreement provided that the agencies would work together to schedule examinations, share information, and avoid issuing conflicting supervisory directives.[25]

At the beginning of the fiscal year, the OCC processed consumer complaints relating to large banks on the CFPB's behalf while the CFPB developed internal systems capable of processing such complaints independently. This process is now complete; the CFPB is processing all consumer complaints under its jurisdiction except for mortgage foreclosure

[25] Office of the Comptroller of the Currency, "Agencies Sign Memorandum of Understanding on Supervisory Coordination," news release 2012-85, June 4, 2012, www.occ.gov.

complaints submitted against banks with more than $10 billion in total assets operating under the mortgage foreclosure consent order. Throughout 2012, the OCC's Customer Assistance Group continued to process questions and complaints relating to consumer issues within the OCC's purview, which includes the BSA, the CRA, flood insurance rules, and all consumer protection issues relating to banks with less than $10 billion in assets.

The importance of interagency collaboration was highlighted in a number of joint actions taken in 2012 to protect consumers from unscrupulous and illegal practices. In coordination with the U.S. Department of Justice, the OCC took enforcement actions against two large national banks for violations and compliance deficiencies related to the SCRA, the law that provides certain financial protections to active-duty servicemembers. OCC examiners found that the two banks had violated a number of SCRA provisions—for example, by denying legitimate claims for interest rate relief under SCRA and pursuing credit card and mortgage judgments against SCRA-covered individuals. The OCC's actions required the banks to engage an independent firm to identify servicemembers who were eligible for SCRA benefits or protections and did not receive them, and to make restitution to them. This case also illustrated the importance of adequate control of third-party vendors, which the two banks had engaged to market and service some of the consumer products connected with the SCRA violations.[26]

An OCC action against another large national bank for violations of section 5 of the Federal Trade Commission Act, which bans "unfair or deceptive acts or practices," was undertaken in collaboration with the CFPB. The bank was cited for abuses in the sale and marketing of products that purported to provide debt cancellation, debt suspension, and credit and identity protection services. Through the bank's own agents and through third-party vendors retained by the bank, customers were subjected to high-pressure sales and retention tactics as well as false and misleading claims

about the benefits these products provided. The OCC imposed a $35 million CMP against the bank and, together with the CFPB, ordered the bank to provide $150 million in restitution to the approximately 2.5 million consumers who were affected by the bank's practices.[27]

In another example of interagency cooperation on behalf of consumers, the OCC worked with the Justice Department in taking action against a large national bank for violations of the federal fair lending laws. The bank was charged with a pattern of discrimination in which African-American and Hispanic borrowers were allegedly steered to higher-priced subprime loans between 2004 and 2008. As a result of the agencies' investigations, the Justice Department was able to enter into a settlement whereby the bank agreed to pay $175 million in compensation, provide assistance to borrowers, and conduct an internal review of its retail mortgage lending, providing additional compensation to minority borrowers as appropriate. The OCC's investigation and the Justice Department's action, Comptroller Curry said, "should send a strong message to every institution that lending discrimination in all its forms will not be tolerated."[28]

Implementing Dodd–Frank

In 2012, the OCC made substantial progress toward meeting Dodd–Frank's requirements, issuing a final rule to remove references to credit ratings from OCC regulations, a rule on stress testing by financial institutions over $10 billion, a proposed rule on appraisals for higher-risk mortgage loans, an interim final rule on lending limits for derivative and securities financing transactions, and a proposed rule on proprietary trading (the Volcker rule). As noted previously, working arrangements between the federal banking agencies and the new CFPB were coordinated and refined. The integration of the personnel, functions, assets, and policies of the former OTS into the OCC continued beyond the July 21, 2011, transfer date. Also, through its outreach and oversight

---

[26] Office of the Comptroller of the Currency, "OCC Takes Actions Against Capital One to Assure Servicemembers Receive Credit Protections for Their Mortgages and Other Loans," news release 2012-115, July 26, 2012, www.occ.gov.

[27] Office of the Comptroller of the Currency, "OCC Assesses Civil Money Penalty Against Capital One, Orders Restitution to 2.5 Million Customers," news release 2012-110, July 18, 2012, www.occ.gov.

[28] Office of the Comptroller of the Currency, "Comptroller Statement Regarding Wells Fargo Fair Lending Settlement," news release 2012-107, July 12, 2012, www.occ.gov.

Strengthening Bank Capital and Harmonizing Capital Standards

The rebuilding of the banking system since the financial crisis has in large part been a story of rising bank capital—a bank's cushion against unexpected losses. Since 2009, the ratio of capital to total assets for banks has grown by nearly 40 percent, boosting confidence in the strength and capability of these institutions to continue serving customers and communities.

The central importance of bank capital to safety and soundness has been the subject of a series of policy pronouncements from various quarters since the financial crisis began. The G20 governments, the Financial Stability Board, the Basel Committee on Banking Supervision, and other international bodies have developed and introduced principles and standards to increase capital.

While embracing much of the international capital agenda, Dodd–Frank added requirements that cause the capital regime applicable to U.S. banks to differ in some respects from those of other countries. One difference, discussed elsewhere in this report, relates to the role of credit ratings in evaluating creditworthiness. Another Dodd–Frank provision, known as the Collins Amendment, requires that minimum capital standards apply to bank holding companies as well as to banks, and that large banks must face capital requirements that are no less stringent than smaller banks.[29]

The federal banking agencies, including the OCC, worked in 2012 to reconcile the provisions of Dodd–Frank with those of the third iteration of the Basel Committee's international capital standards. In June the OCC and other federal banking agencies issued three notices of proposed rulemaking (NPR) concerning implementation of the various capital rules for U.S. banks.[30] In the first NPR, the agencies proposed to adopt the new Basel III minimum capital requirement, based on common equity, the strongest kind of capital. In addition, the agencies proposed to limit dividend and compensation payouts if a bank does not hold equity capital beyond certain threshold amounts relative to risk-weighted assets.

In the second NPR, the agencies proposed to revise and harmonize rules for calculating risk-weighted assets in order to enhance risk sensitivity and address weaknesses identified in recent years. These proposed revisions would be applicable to all banking organizations.

In the third NPR, the federal banking agencies proposed to adopt certain aspects of the Basel III framework as it applies to the largest and most complex organizations.

In recognition of the substantial changes to the regulatory capital framework that had been proposed, and to facilitate comment from and understanding by smaller banks, the OCC, in conjunction with the other banking agencies, undertook efforts to ease the burden of analyzing the proposed rules. For example, the banking agencies separated the proposals into the three NPRs noted above so that smaller banks could disregard the third NPR in its entirety. In addition, the agencies developed addendums to the first two NPRs summarizing them for smaller banks and identifying the elements that would apply to those institutions. The agencies also built an estimator tool to help smaller banks assess the amount of capital that might be needed to comply with the proposed standards. Finally, the OCC and the other agencies also conducted extensive outreach in a variety of forums and extended the comment period to allow the industry more time to assess and comment on the proposals.

---

[29] Statement of John Walsh, Committee on Banking, Housing, and Urban Affairs, U.S. Senate, March 22, 2012, www.occ.gov.

[30] Office of the Comptroller of the Currency, "Agencies Seek Comment on Regulatory Capital Rules and Finalize Market Risk Rule," news release 2012-88, June 12, 2012, www.occ.gov.

Rule on Risk-Based Capital for Market Risk

In 1988, the Basel Committee, the body that serves as a forum for international cooperation on bank supervisory matters, promulgated the first international agreement on bank capital standards. Eight years later, in 1996, the committee developed additional standards on capital requirements for market risk—those risks to a bank's trading activities that arise from fluctuations in interest rates, currency exchange rates, and commodity and stock market prices. The Basel Committee refined these standards after the financial crisis revealed weaknesses in market-risk management, and it boosted the capital standards for market risk.[31]

The OCC and other U.S. banking agencies largely adopted the new Basel standards in developing a final rule on risk-based capital for market risk. The OCC rule applies to banks with trading assets and liabilities that are more than 10 percent of total assets or more than $1 billion. In accordance with Dodd–Frank, U.S. banks may not use external credit ratings to calculate their capital charge for market risk.[32]

The final rule incorporates a revised definition of the trading positions subject to the market-risk capital charge and to requirements that affected banks adopt more rigorous stress testing of covered positions, improved internal models, and higher disclosure standards. The rule goes into effect on January 1, 2013.[33]

activities, the OCC's Office of Minority and Women Inclusion, another Dodd–Frank initiative, promoted diversity in the workplace, in the ranks of OCC contractors, and among OCC-regulated institutions.

In all, the OCC undertook more than 100 projects to conform to the new law, either separately or with other agencies.

Rule on Credit Ratings

Banks have long been permitted to purchase "investment grade" bonds and other debt instruments for their own investment accounts. Over the years, banks and regulators came to rely heavily on evaluations by credit-rating agencies to determine whether the investments under consideration were safe to hold. Unfortunately, during the financial crisis, many highly rated securities, particularly private-label, mortgage-backed securities, performed poorly, and some ratings agencies gave dubious mortgage-backed securities higher ratings than they deserved, leaving institutional and other investors with big losses. That experience prompted section 939A of Dodd–Frank, which required regulators to modify their definition of "investment grade" to remove references to credit ratings. As a result, the revised rule requires banks to undertake more comprehensive evaluations of the quality of securities being considered for investment.

On June 26, 2012, the OCC issued a final rule on credit ratings, removing from its regulations all requirements that banks consider external credit ratings in making an "investment grade" determination. "In other words," the rule states, "a security rated in the top four rating categories by [a nationally recognized statistical rating organization] is not automatically deemed to satisfy the revised 'investment grade' standard." Banks may continue using agency ratings in performing their evaluations, however, to supplement their internal credit risk management processes and other third-party analytical tools.[34]

To facilitate this transition, the OCC simultaneously released final guidance as an aid to banks, particularly community banks and federal savings associations, regarding the factors they should consider in their due diligence when assessing securities of different degrees of complexity. The OCC understands that many smaller banks have lacked the capacity to perform the kind of independent credit analysis that the regulation requires, and the guidance provides those institutions with a number of tools to assist them, including a matrix of factors to consider when banks perform these self-assessments.[35]

---

[31] Basel Committee on Banking Supervision, "Revisions to the Basel II Market Risk Framework," February 2011, www.bis.org/publ/bcbs193.htm.

[32] Office of the Comptroller of the Currency, "Regulatory Capital-Basel III and the Standardized and Advanced Approaches: Notice of Proposed Rulemaking," bulletin 2012-24, August 30, 2012, www.occ.gov.

[33] Testimony of Thomas J. Curry, Committee on Banking, Housing, and Urban Affairs, U.S. Senate, June 6, 2012, www.occ.gov.

[34] Office of the Comptroller of the Currency, "Alternatives to the Use of External Credit Ratings in the Regulations of the OCC: Final Rules and Guidance," bulletin 2012-18, June 26, 2012, www.occ.gov.

[35] Ibid.

Rule on Stress Testing

The financial crisis proved the value of rigorous, credible stress tests, such as those conducted in 2009 under the auspices of the Supervisory Capital Assessment Program.[36] These tests can help banks identify weaknesses, withstand adversity, and maintain public confidence.

Dodd–Frank requires annual stress testing in institutions with assets of $10 billion to $50 billion and twice-annual stress testing for banks that exceed $50 billion. It further requires the primary regulator of financial institutions subject to the stress testing requirement to issue regulations that implement the stress test requirements, define the methods for stress testing, and set standards for the reporting and publication of each institution's stress test results.

In October 2012, the OCC and the other federal banking agencies released the Dodd–Frank-mandated stress test rule. The implementation timeline calls for the largest banks to implement stress testing immediately, while banks with $10 billion to $50 billion in assets, which generally have less experience with stress testing, are afforded a full year before stress testing must begin.[37]

In addition, the OCC and the other federal banking agencies issued guidance in May 2012 that discussed the uses and merits of stress testing in specific areas of risk management for banks with assets greater than $10 billion. The guidance outlines the general principles of a satisfactory stress testing framework and describes how banks should implement them. The guidance also discusses the importance of stress testing in capital and liquidity planning and the importance of strong internal governance.[38] The agencies noted that while the guidance and Dodd–Frank stress testing rules do not apply to banks with less than $10 billion in assets, all banking organizations, regardless of size, should have the capacity to analyze the potential

impact of adverse outcomes on their financial condition in a manner consistent with the institution's risk profile.[39]

Rule on Lending Limits

In general, the OCC's lending limits rule imposes specified limits on national bank and federal savings association loans and extensions of credit to one borrower. Section 610 of Dodd–Frank expanded the definition of loans and extensions of credit to include certain derivative instruments, repurchase agreements, reverse repurchase agreements, and securities lending or borrowing transactions. The goal is to better regulate the large over-the-counter derivatives market.[40]

In June 2012, the OCC adopted an interim final rule that amended its lending limit rule to implement Section 610. The rule provided a compliance date of January 1, 2013, to give banks time to adapt to the new standard. The rule provides different options for measuring the exposure of each transaction type, which are intended to reduce the regulatory burden for midsize and community banks.[41]

---

[36] For an account of the Supervisory Capital Assessment Program, see the OCC's *Annual Report FY 2009*, 11–12, www.occ.gov.

[37] Office of the Comptroller of the Currency, "Comptroller Curry's Statement Regarding FDIC Stress Test Rule," news release 2012-143, October 9, 2012, www.occ.gov.

[38] Office of the Comptroller of the Currency, "Agencies Finalize Large Bank Stress Testing Guidance," news release 2012-75, May 14, 2012, www.occ.gov.

[39] Office of the Comptroller of the Currency, "Statement to Clarify Supervisory Expectations for Stress Testing by Community Banks," May 14, 2012, www.occ.gov.

[40] Office of the Comptroller of the Currency, "OCC Issues an Interim Final Lending Limit Rule," news release 2012-92, June 20, 2012, www.occ.gov.

[41] Office of the Comptroller of the Currency, "Lending Limits: Interim Final Rule," bulletin 2012-19, June 29, 2012, www.occ.gov. It is anticipated that the compliance date will be extended when the final rule is adopted.

The Volcker Rule

Section 619 of Dodd–Frank, known as the Volcker rule, prohibits banks from engaging in short-term proprietary trading of securities and derivatives for the banks' own account. It also prohibits banks from owning or having certain relationships with hedge funds or private equity funds.

In developing and implementing regulations, the OCC and other federal agencies had to consider how to distinguish impermissible proprietary trading from permitted market-making-related activities, hedging, underwriting, and transactions on behalf of customers. A second important issue was how to identify the hedge funds and private equity funds that would be covered by the Volcker rule, including whether some kinds of securitization would be considered "hedge funds" and thus subject to Volcker rule restrictions.[42]

These complex questions led to a proposed rulemaking that was released for public comment on October 11, 2011. Running to almost 300 pages, the proposal included nearly 400 questions on issues still to be resolved.[43] In light of public interest in the proposal, the federal banking agencies agreed to extend the deadline for comments for one month, from January to February 2012.[44] More than 19,000

comment letters were received by the closing date. The agencies are now discussing the issues raised by commenters and are drafting revisions to the proposal. Financial institutions will have two years, or until July 21, 2014, at the latest, to conform their activities to the statutory prohibitions and any final rule that is issued, unless an extension is granted by the Federal Reserve.[45]

Questions about the scope of the Volcker rule were highlighted by events at the nation's largest bank, JP Morgan Chase (JPMC). In late April and early May, JPMC experienced large losses that resulted from a sudden deterioration of positions taken by the bank that began as a program to hedge against credit risk. These losses prompted a comprehensive review of the adequacy and rigor of the bank's risk management practices and of the OCC's oversight of the bank. The events also raised questions about whether the activities in question would have been prohibited activities under section 619 of Dodd–Frank.

During congressional hearings on June 6, Comptroller Curry discussed the OCC's ongoing review of its supervision of JPMC and the relationship between JPMC's difficulties and the Volcker rule.[46]

Transfer of the Former OTS

On July 21, 2011, under the authority of Title III of Dodd–Frank, most functions of the OTS transferred to the OCC. From that day forward, the OCC has been responsible for the examination, supervision, and regulation of federal savings associations.

Important work remained to be done in 2012 to finalize the transfer of personnel, functions, and assets. The integration of OCC and OTS regulations and the merger of more than 1,000 OTS supervisory policies into a consolidated OCC policy framework continued, with the goal of eliminating duplication, reducing unnecessary burden, and providing consistent treatment, where appropriate, for both national banks and federal savings associations.[47]

[42] Statement of John Walsh, Acting Comptroller of the Currency, Subcommittees on Capital Markets and Government Sponsored Enterprises and on Financial Institutions and Consumer Credit, Committee on Financial Services, U.S. House of Representatives, January 18, 2012, www.occ.gov.

[43] Office of the Comptroller of the Currency, "The OCC Issues Volcker Rule Proposal for Public Comment," news release 2011-126, October 11, 2011, www.occ.gov.

[44] Office of the Comptroller of the Currency, "Agencies Extend Comment Period on Volcker Rule Proposal," news release 2011-155, December 23, 2011, www.occ.gov.

[45] Office of the Comptroller of the Currency, "Volcker Rule Conformance Period Clarified," news release 2012-64, April 19, 2012, www.occ.gov.

[46] Statement of Thomas J. Curry, Committee on Banking, Housing, and Urban Affairs, U.S. Senate, June 6, 2012, www.occ.gov.

[47] Testimony of John Walsh, Committee on Banking, Housing, and Urban Affairs, U.S. Senate, December 6, 2011, www.occ.gov.

As part of this process, the OCC rescinded hundreds of OTS documents that were outdated, were replaced, or are being incorporated into OCC supervisory publications.[48]

The OCC recognized from the beginning that these changes would usher in a period of uncertainty for federal savings associations now operating under the OCC's authority. To help those institutions understand and adapt to changes in their regulation and supervision, the agency held a number of outreach meetings and teleconferences at which concerns were aired and explanations provided by OCC supervisory staff.[49]

Office of Minority and Women Inclusion

In 2012, the OCC continued to rank near the top among the "Best Places to Work in the Federal Government," with especially strong scores from employees for the OCC's support for diversity.

Section 342 of Dodd–Frank reinforced the agency's diversity objectives by requiring each of the federal banking agencies to establish an Office of Minority and Women Inclusion (OMWI). The office's mandate is to develop standards for equal employment opportunity and racial, ethnic, and gender diversity among the workforce and senior management of the agency; increase participation among minority- and women-owned businesses with which the agency contracts; and assess the diversity policies and practices of the financial institutions that they supervise and regulate.

In March, the OCC OMWI documented its activities in a report to Congress. The office continued to focus its activities in 2012 on increasing the participation of Hispanics in OCC major occupations and of women in the national bank examiner positions, two areas in which their workforce participation falls below the National Civilian Labor Force comparator for those occupational groups. The OCC continued to support

Joyce Cofield, Executive Director of the OCC's Office of Minority and Women Inclusion (right), speaks with an attendee during an outreach event for minority small-business contractors.

minority and female high school and college students for internship opportunities.

To promote opportunities for minority- and women-owned businesses, the OCC enhanced its outreach program by creating print publications and enabling electronic access to information about the OMWI program and how to conduct business with the agency. The OCC's OMWI also increased its attendance at vendor forums throughout the country to engage in one-on-one discussions with and provide technical assistance to minority- and women-owned businesses. For FY 2011 and FY 2012, the OCC awarded procurement actions representing 38 percent and 34 percent, respectively, of its total spending to minority- and women-owned businesses.

Perhaps the most challenging part of section 342 of Dodd–Frank is its mandate that OMWI develop standards for assessing the diversity policies and practices of entities regulated by the OCC. The OCC is working collaboratively with its counterparts at the other federal banking agencies to develop consistent and appropriate standards for the diversity assessments. The OMWI interagency group has held a series of roundtable meetings with industry representatives and trade and consumer advocacy groups around the country to solicit input and gather information on best approaches for implementing this section of Dodd–Frank.[50] The interagency group is developing a notice for publication in the *Federal*

[48] Office of the Comptroller of the Currency, "Rescission of OTS Documents," bulletin 2012-2, January 6, 2012, www.occ.gov; bulletin 2012-15, May 17, 2012, www.occ.gov; bulletin 2012-23, August 24, 2012, www.occ.gov.

[49] See, for example, Office of the Comptroller of the Currency, "Office of the Comptroller of the Currency Hosts Workshops in New Jersey," news release 2012-21, February 10, 2012, www.occ.gov. Twelve such workshops were held in 2012.

[50] "Office of Minority and Women Inclusion, Section 342, 2011 Annual Report to Congress, March 2012," www.occ.gov.

Register to enable interested parties to provide comments on the proposed standards.

A key related goal is to sustain a viable minority-owned banking sector, which was hit especially hard during the economic recession. The OCC has long recognized the importance of minority-owned banks, which often play a vital role in providing financial services to underserved communities. To help the agency understand the unique challenges these institutions face, the OCC is in the process of establishing an advisory committee on minority banks, which will be made up of officers and directors of those institutions and other financial institutions committed to supporting them. Committee members will offer insights to OCC supervisory personnel on providing technical assistance, encouraging the formation of new minority financial institutions, and safeguarding the minority character of these institutions during mergers or acquisitions.[51]

Comptroller Curry speaks about the importance of small-business lending to economic growth and job creation.

---

[51] Office of the Comptroller of the Currency, "OCC Establishes Advisory Committees on Minority Institutions and Mutual Associations," news release 2011-131, October 21, 2011, www.occ.gov.

Section Two
Condition of the Federal Banking System

Summary

Profitability at banks improved in the first half of calendar year 2012[52] but remains below its two-decade average. With loan demand still weak, the substitution of lower-yielding securities for higher-yielding loans continued to compress net interest margins. Expenses due to provisions for loan losses declined again from year-earlier levels and are below their long-run average as a percentage of loans. Credit quality continued to improve, as net charge-off rates fell for all major loan categories.

Discussion

For the first half of calendar year 2012, net income at OCC-supervised banks increased by $6.6 billion compared with the first half of 2011. Quarterly net income is running at about the same level as five years ago. Profitability, as measured by return on equity, stood at 8.8 percent for the second quarter and above the level of a year earlier. With system assets $1 trillion higher than five years ago, and with banks holding more capital, return on equity is still well below the level achieved then.

Credit quality and provisions. Credit quality has improved steadily over the past three years. Charge-off rates declined for all major loan categories in the first half of 2012 compared with a year earlier.

Despite the generally improved credit performance, loss rates have remained high for residential real estate, due in part to the backlog of foreclosed properties. Moreover, an estimated 20 percent of all first-lien mortgages exceed the current value of the homes financed, with much higher shares in the hardest hit states, such as Arizona, Florida, and Nevada.

A number of factors may have delayed the usual foreclosure process. For example, while loan modification programs may avert foreclosure in some cases, in other cases mortgage loans proceed to foreclosure despite modification. As a result, some future foreclosures may simply be postponed rather than avoided. These forces make it unlikely that loss rates will soon return to pre-crisis levels. For commercial real estate loans, charge-off rates have begun to fall, but fundamental performance measures such as vacancy rates are still lagging.

OCC-supervised banks have set aside less in reserves for future losses. Loan-loss provisions fell by $7.3 billion in the first half of 2012 compared with a year earlier and are below their long-run average as a share of total loans.

Revenues. Pre-provision net revenues edged up 1 percent in the first half of 2012 compared with the same period a year earlier. The weak economy continues to pressure net interest margins, as loans mature and are replaced by low-yielding cash and securities.

Relatively weak economic growth combined with deleveraging by consumers is constraining loan demand, suggesting that banks are unlikely to see a return to pre-crisis growth rates in consumer lending anytime soon. Lending grew 2 percent in the first half of 2012, compared with a year earlier. Corporate

---

[52] Only data for the first half of calendar year 2012 were available by publication deadline. Note: Fair value adjustments had a material influence on reported results.

profits have recovered to pre-recession levels, but with many firms accumulating cash, and even medium-size firms now able to access the bond markets, banks have experienced less growth in business lending than they did during previous recoveries.

Growing revenue has been more of a challenge for smaller banks than for larger banks because smaller banks did not benefit as much from the sharp drop in interest rates in 2008, following the onset of the recession.

Noninterest expenses rose sharply in the first half of 2012; this increase, however, was driven by results at one large bank and overstates changes in noninterest expenses across banks generally. Noninterest income grew modestly in the first half of 2012 compared with a year earlier, in part from increased loan sales. This growth in noninterest income was more than enough to offset the increase in expenses and the weakness in interest income, pushing net income growth into positive territory.

Funding. Business and retail deposits rose sharply during the financial crisis, as other investments appeared less attractive and savers turned to banks for safety. Businesses in particular have accounted for a significant surge in checkable deposits since 2008. Large banks have been the main recipients of these deposit flows, which have helped hold down their funding costs; this pattern continued in 2012. Although these deposits offer low-cost funding, they may be harder for banks to retain if returns increase on alternatives to bank deposits.

Section Three
OCC Organization

Thomas J. Curry
Comptroller of the Currency

Thomas J. Curry was sworn in as the 30th Comptroller of the Currency on April 9, 2012, replacing John Walsh, who had served as Acting Comptroller since August 15, 2010.

The Comptroller of the Currency is the chief executive of the OCC, which supervises national banks and federal savings associations and the federal branches and agencies of foreign banks in the United States. The Comptroller also is a director of the FDIC and NeighborWorks America.

Before becoming Comptroller of the Currency, Mr. Curry was a Director of the FDIC from 2004 to 2012. Mr. Curry served five Massachusetts governors as the Commonwealth's Commissioner of Banks from 1990 to 1991 and again from 1995 to 2003. He entered state government in 1982 as an attorney with the Massachusetts Office of the Secretary of State.

Mr. Curry was chairman of the Conference of State Bank Supervisors from 2000 to 2001 and served two terms on the State Liaison Committee of the Federal Financial Institutions Examination Council, including a term as its chairman.

He is a summa cum laude graduate of Manhattan College, where he was elected to Phi Beta Kappa. He received his law degree from the New England School of Law.

Executive Committee

Thomas J. Curry
Comptroller of the Currency

Paul M. Nash
Senior Deputy Comptroller and
Chief of Staff

John C. Lyons Jr.
Senior Deputy Comptroller for
Bank Supervision Policy and
Chief National Bank Examiner

Michael L. Brosnan
Senior Deputy Comptroller for
Large Bank Supervision

Jennifer C. Kelly
Senior Deputy Comptroller for
Midsize and Community Bank
Supervision

Julie L. Williams
First Senior Deputy Comptroller
and Chief Counsel

Mark Levonian
Senior Deputy Comptroller for
Economics

Thomas R. Bloom
Senior Deputy Comptroller
for Management and Chief
Financial Officer

Chief of Staff

Paul M. Nash, Senior Deputy Comptroller and Chief of Staff, oversees the external affairs and communication functions of the OCC, including Congressional Liaison, Banking Relations, Press Relations, Internal Communications, Minority Affairs, and Communications, and directs the daily operations of the Comptroller's support staff. Mr. Nash joined the OCC in this role in May 2012.

Mr. Nash was the Deputy to the Chairman for External Affairs at the FDIC from 2009 to 2012. He served as Executive Director and Counsel at Verizon Wireless in Washington, D.C., from 2001 to 2009. Before joining Verizon Wireless, Mr. Nash was a legislative assistant to Senator Tim Johnson (D-S.D.) from 1997 to 2001. He also worked for the Congressional Research Service and practiced law in Washington, D.C., and New Orleans, La.

Mr. Nash received a bachelor of arts degree in international relations and history from the University of Pennsylvania and a law degree from Georgetown University.

Chief National Bank Examiner's Office

As Senior Deputy Comptroller for Bank Supervision Policy and Chief National Bank Examiner, John C. Lyons Jr. oversees the development of supervisory policies and examination procedures and tools in the areas of bank information technology, capital, commercial and retail credit risk, compliance, financial markets, balance sheet and asset management, and operational risk. The department includes the Office of the Chief Accountant, which is responsible for accounting policy guidance for national banks and federal savings associations, and oversees the OCC's NRC.

Mr. Lyons joined the OCC in 1977 as an Assistant National Bank Examiner and has held a variety of leadership and staff positions in bank supervision as a field examiner, a credit team leader, and Examiner-in-Charge of several banks. He earned a bachelor of science degree in business administration from DePaul University and a master's degree in business administration from Loyola University Chicago.

Large Bank Supervision

The Department of Large Bank Supervision is headed by Senior Deputy Comptroller Michael L. Brosnan. The department oversees the supervision of the largest and most complex national banks and federal savings associations as well as foreign-owned U.S. branches and agencies.

Mr. Brosnan joined the OCC in 1983 and received his commission as a National Bank Examiner in 1986. His previous OCC positions include Deputy Comptroller for Large Bank Supervision, Examiner-in-Charge, Deputy Comptroller for Risk Evaluation, and Director of Treasury and Market Risk. He also worked as a risk manager at MBNA and then Bank of America from 2004 to 2008. He holds a bachelor of arts degree and a master's degree in business administration from Lynchburg College.

Midsize and Community Bank Supervision

Senior Deputy Comptroller Jennifer C. Kelly oversees the Midsize and Community Bank Supervision Department. The department is responsible for the supervision of midsize and community banks, focusing on ensuring sound risk identification and management processes and regulatory compliance.

Ms. Kelly joined the OCC in 1979 as an Assistant National Bank Examiner and received her commission in 1983. She has a broad supervision background, including extensive experience in problem bank supervision and policy development. She earned a bachelor of arts degree in economics from Mount Holyoke College.

Chief Counsel's Office

First Senior Deputy Comptroller and Chief Counsel Julie L. Williams supervises the OCC's Law, Licensing, and Community Affairs departments.

The Law Department enforces compliance with banking requirements and securities laws, addresses protection and fair treatment of bank customers through enforcement of consumer laws and regulations, issues opinions on national bank powers and activities, handles OCC litigation matters, provides legislative analysis and technical advice, and develops regulations. The Licensing Department charters national banks and federal savings associations and issues decisions on regulated institution structure and business changes. The Community Affairs Department supports national banks and federal savings associations in their community development activities and the provision of financial services to underserved communities and consumers.

Ms. Williams joined the OCC as Deputy Chief Counsel in 1993 after years of experience in the private sector and at the OTS and its predecessor, the Federal Home Loan Bank Board. She became OCC Chief Counsel in 1994. Ms. Williams has a bachelor of arts degree from Goddard College and a law degree from the Antioch School of Law. She announced her retirement from the OCC effective December 31, 2012.

Economics

The Economics Department is directed by Senior Deputy Comptroller Mark Levonian. The department provides economic analysis of national and global economic trends, provides on-site and off-site examination support for bank supervision, contributes to policy development, and conducts original research to support the OCC's mission.

Mr. Levonian held a succession of positions in the Federal Reserve System before joining the OCC in 2004 as Deputy Comptroller for Modeling and Analysis. He holds a bachelor's degree in economics from the University of California at Berkeley and a Ph.D. in economics from the Massachusetts Institute of Technology.

Office of Management

The Office of Management is led by Thomas R. Bloom, the Senior Deputy Comptroller for Management and Chief Financial Officer. The office administers the OCC's human resources, asset acquisition, travel and staff relocation, physical space, training and development, physical and personnel security, compensation and benefits, and financial management. It also provides the OCC's information technology services.

Mr. Bloom's extensive government career has included positions in the U.S. Departments of Defense, Commerce, and Education and the General Services Administration. He came to the OCC in his current position in 2003. Mr. Bloom has a bachelor's degree in business administration from the University of Michigan and is a certified public accountant.

Ombudsman

Larry L. Hattix

The Office of the Ombudsman administers the national bank appeals program, the OCC's Customer Assistance Group, and the Enterprise Governance unit. The office, headed by Larry L. Hattix, reports directly to the Comptroller of the Currency.

Mr. Hattix joined the OCC as an Assistant National Bank Examiner in 1988 after graduating with a bachelor's degree in business administration and finance from Carroll College. He received his commission as a National Bank Examiner in 1994, with a specialization in consumer and CRA compliance.

Office of Minority and Women Inclusion

Joyce Cofield

OMWI, headed by Executive Director Joyce Cofield, is responsible for developing standards for equal employment opportunity and the racial, ethnic, and gender diversity of the OCC's workforce and senior management; increasing the participation of minority- and women-owned businesses in the OCC's programs and contracts; and assessing the diversity policies and practices of the OCC's regulated entities. The office reports directly to the Comptroller of the Currency.

Before joining the OCC in 2001 as Director of Employment and Diversity Management, Ms. Cofield held a number of leadership roles at the Polaroid Corporation. She holds a bachelor of science degree in biology from Virginia Union University and a master's degree in industrial microbiology from Boston University.

Section Four
Licensing and Enforcement Measures

Figure 1: Corporate Application Activity, FY 2011 and FY 2012

	FY 2011[a]	FY 2012	FY 2012 decisions			
	Applications received		Approved	Conditionally approved	Denied	Total[b]
Branches	917	844	860	2	0	862
Capital/sub-debt	224	174	142	2	0	145
Change in bank control	4	10	1	2	0	6
Charters	6	2	1	1	0	2
Conversions[c]	8	5	2	6	0	8
Federal branches	2	5	0	2	0	2
Fiduciary powers	9	16	3	2	0	5
Mergers[d]	70	98	86	6	0	94
Relocations	187	197	191	1	0	192
Reorganizations (national banks only)	71	53	43	6	0	49
Stock appraisals	0	0	0	0	0	0
Subsidiaries	107	148	112	2	0	115
12 CFR 5.53 change in assets	2	26	22	5	0	27
Limited national bank upgrade	1	0	0	0	0	0
Operations	31	35	25	0	0	25
Sasser/conversions out[e]	9	38	41	0	0	41
Bylaw/charter (federal savings associations only)	8	73	66	0	0	66
Total	**1,656**	**1,724**	**1,595**	**37**	**0**	**1,639**

Source: OCC data.

[a] Data collected for federal savings associations are for the fourth quarter of FY 2011 only.

[b] Total includes alternative decisions or no-objections.

[c] Conversions to national bank charters.

[d] Mergers include failure transactions when a national bank is the resulting institution.

[e] Conversions to federal savings association charters and mutual-to-stock conversions.

Figure 2: Licensing Actions and Timeliness, FY 2011 and FY 2012

| | Target time frames in days[a] | FY 2011 | | | FY 2012 | | |
| | | Number of decisions | Within target | | Number of decisions | Within target | |
			Number	Percent		Number	Percent
Branches	45/60	870	857	99	862	858	100
Capital/sub-debt	30/45	185	176	95	145	142	98
Change in bank control	NA/60	3	2	67	6	5	83
Charters[b]		8	7	88	2	2	100
Conversions	30/90	3	2	67	8	6	75
Federal branches	NA/120	1	1	100	2	2	100
Fiduciary powers	30/45	2	2	100	5	4	80
Mergers	45/60	51	49	96	94	91	97
Relocations	45/60	170	165	97	192	188	98
Reorganizations	45/60	64	58	91	49	42	86
Stock appraisals	NA/90	0	0	0	0	0	0
Subsidiaries	NA	24	21	88	115	113	98
12 CFR 5.53 change in assets	NA/60	1	1	100	27	26	96
Limited national bank upgrade		0	0	0	0	0	0
Operations	30/60				25	25	100
Sasser/conversions out	30/60				41	41	100
Bylaw/charter	30/60				66	66	100
Total		**1,382**	**1,341**	**97**	**1,639**	**1,611**	**98**

Source: OCC data.

Note: Most decisions (97 percent in 2011 and 93 percent in 2012) were decided in the district offices and Large Bank Licensing under delegated authority. Decisions include approvals, conditional approvals, and denials. NA means not applicable.

[a] The data are for national banks and federal savings associations combined. Those filings that qualified for the "expedited review" process are subject to the shorter time frames listed. The longer time frames are the standard benchmarks for more complex applications. The target time frame may be extended if the OCC needs additional information to reach a decision, permits additional time for public comment, or processes a group of related filings as one transaction.

[b] For independent national bank charter applications, the target time frame is 120 days. For holding-company-sponsored applications, the target time frame is 45 days for applications eligible for expedited review and 90 days for all others.

Figure 3: OCC Changes in Bank Control Act Actions, FY 2008–FY 2012 (Notices Processed With Disposition)[a]

Year	Received	Acted on	Not disapproved	Disapproved	Withdrawn
2012	10	6	6	0	0
2011	4	6	6	0	0
2010	8	5	5	0	0
2009	10	10	7	0	3
2008	5	4	4	0	0

Source: OCC data.

[a] FY 2011 and 2012 data are for national banks and federal savings associations combined.

Figure 4: OCC Enforcement Actions, FY 2012

Type of enforcement action	Against institutions	Against institution-affiliated parties
Cease-and-desist orders	57	9
Temporary cease-and-desist orders	0	0
12 USC 1818 civil money penalties	2	38
12 USC 1818 civil money penalties amount assessed	$ 55,000,000	$ 220,250
Flood insurance civil money penalties	8	0
Flood insurance civil money penalties amount assessed	$ 111,775	$ 0
Restitution orders	4	2
Amount of restitution ordered	$ 164,518,013	$ 37,000
Formal agreements	57	0
Capital directives	0	NA
Prompt corrective action directives	8	NA
Individual minimum capital ratio letters	46	NA
Safety and soundness orders	0	NA
Memorandums of understanding	29	0
Commitment letters	2	NA
Suspension orders	NA	1
12 USC 1818 removal/prohibition orders	NA	19
12 USC 1829 prohibitions	NA	103
Letters of reprimand	NA	10
Total	**213**	**182**

Note: NA means not applicable.

Figure 5: List of Applications Presenting Community Reinvestment Act Issues Decided, FY 2012

Bank, city, state	Approval date	Document number
Raymond James Bank, FSB, St. Petersburg, Fla. (conversion)	January 2012	Conditional Approval No. 1022
Capital One, NA, and Capital One Bank (USA), NA, McLean, Va. (purchase and assumption)	March 2012	CRA Decision No. 149
First Niagara Bank, NA, Buffalo, N.Y. (purchase and assumption)	April 2012	Conditional Approval No. 1031
TD Bank, NA, Wilmington, Del. (branch establishment)	August 2012	CRA Decision No. 150

Section Five
Financial Management Discussion and Analysis

Letter From the Chief Financial Officer

I am pleased to present the OCC's financial statements as an integral part of the *Fiscal Year 2012 Annual Report*. For FY 2012, our independent auditors have again rendered an unqualified opinion with no material internal control weaknesses. The financial statements include the assets and liabilities transferred to the OCC from the OTS on July 21, 2011, as required by Dodd–Frank, and are presented in accordance with generally accepted accounting principles (GAAP).

In FY 2012, the OCC provided unqualified assurance that its internal controls over financial reporting operate effectively and have no material weaknesses in their design or operation. The OCC continuously strives for strong internal controls by implementing the guidance found in the Office of Management and Budget's (OMB) Circular A-123, "Management's Responsibility for Internal Control, Appendix A— Internal Control Over Financial Reporting."

The determination, made by the OCC and required by OMB, was based on the OCC Financial Management Department's detailed, annual risk assessment of the financial statements and rigorous tests of controls. The OCC highly values such an evaluation, as it attests to the agency's strong internal control environment, which has never been more important to the federal government. In fact, the majority of the findings noted in the "Independent Auditor's Report on Internal Control Over Financial Reporting" were self-identified by our internal controls staff, and plans of corrective action already have been implemented for all of the findings.

As a nonappropriated federal agency, the OCC receives the majority of its funding by collecting assessment fees from national banks and federal savings associations. The revenue from these fees is used to fund the OCC's operations. In addition to assessment revenue, the OCC receives interest income on its long-term investments and rental income from the occupancy agreement in place with the CFPB.

Thomas R. Bloom, Senior Deputy Comptroller for Management and Chief Financial Officer

The OCC has long recognized the importance of spending only what is necessary to accomplish its mission. Personnel, contractual services, and rent are the OCC's three leading costs, representing 76 percent of its total annual operating budget. In FY 2012, the OCC incurred a one-time cost of $86.2 million to fully fund the defined benefit pension plan assumed from the OTS. This pension plan, which has not been open to new entrants since 1989, covers 230 current OCC employees and 551 retirees. Dodd–Frank requires that the OCC maintain this plan and be responsible for the ongoing obligation to fund it. After absorbing this and other costs related to the OTS integration, the OCC's overall financial condition remains sound.

At the end of each fiscal year, unused budgetary funds are put into financial reserves. These financial reserves have allowed the OCC to maintain its bank assessment rate structure and, except for annual inflation adjustments, avoid assessment fee increases since 2002. In FY 2012, the asset replacement reserve was utilized to facilitate the consolidation of several office locations in Washington, D.C., into one headquarters building. Leasehold improvements and relocation costs are two of the largest costs involved in this project, which is to be completed in February 2013.

In addition to spending only what is necessary to accomplish its mission, the OCC focuses on reducing costs wherever feasible. To that end, the Office of Management (OM) operates a Lean Six Sigma (LSS) program to ensure that administrative processes are continually reviewed and improved. The LSS program is based on a managerial concept that aims to eliminate seven kinds of waste, referred to as Defects, Overproduction, Transportation, Waiting, Inventory, Motion, and Over-Processing. The program has produced significant cost savings. Since the program's implementation in 2005, 199 LSS projects have been completed with total first-year cost savings or avoidance of $33.6 million. This fiscal year alone, the OCC completed 49 business process improvement or LSS projects resulting in $1.3 million in total cost

savings. All OM executives have received formal LSS training, and the OCC has 60 staff members who are certified as Master Black Belts, Black Belts, or Green Belts and 33 employees who are actively pursuing their certifications.

With the successful integration of the OTS realized, the OCC continues to focus on its core mission: to supervise, regulate, and charter national banks and federal savings associations. The OCC's strong internal controls environment, solid financial resources, and process improvement programs ensure successful operations in FY 2013 and beyond.

Thomas R. Bloom
Senior Deputy Comptroller for Management
and Chief Financial Officer

Financial Summary

The OCC received an unqualified opinion on its FY 2012 and FY 2011 financial statements. The OCC's financial statements consist of Balance Sheets, Statements of Net Cost, Statements of Changes in Net Position, and Statements of Budgetary Resources. The OCC presents the financial statements and notes on a comparative basis, providing financial information for FY 2012 and FY 2011. The financial statements were prepared from the OCC's accounting records in conformity with GAAP. The financial statements include the assets and liabilities that were transferred to the OCC from the OTS on July 21, 2011, the transfer date, as required by Dodd–Frank. The financial statements, followed by notes and the auditor's opinion, begin on page 42.

The following sections of the report address the OCC's financial activities in FY 2012 and FY 2011.

Assets

The OCC's assets include both "entity" and "non-entity" assets. The OCC uses entity assets, which belong to the agency, to fund operations. Non-entity assets are assets that the OCC holds on behalf of another federal agency. The OCC's non-entity assets presented as accounts receivable are CMPs due the federal government through court-enforced legal actions.

As of September 30, 2012, total assets were $1,519.5 million, a decrease of $7.1 million, or 0.5 percent, from the total assets of $1,526.6 million reported on September 30, 2011. Factors contributing to the net reduction in total assets include a decrease of $228.2 million in the fund balance with Treasury (FBWT) used for OCC FY 2012 operating expenses and increases in investments and related interest of $191.8 million and in property and equipment of $31.0 million. The increase in property and equipment resulted primarily from the addition of assets related to the leasehold improvement project and equipment purchases for the OCC's new headquarters building.

Figure 6 shows the OCC's composition of assets for FY 2012 and FY 2011.

Figure 6: Composition of Assets (in Millions)

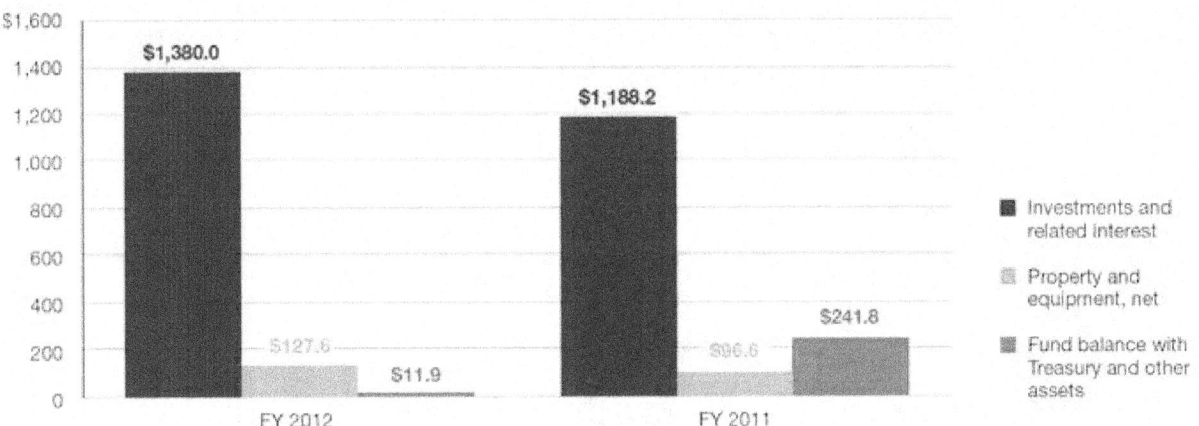

Source: OCC financial system data.

Investments

Investments and related interest on September 30, 2012, were $1,380.0 million, compared with $1,188.2 million a year earlier. The market value of the OCC's investment portfolio in excess of book value rose this year to $40.3 million from $38.9 million on September 30, 2011. The OCC invests available funds in non-marketable U.S. Treasury securities issued through the Treasury Department's Bureau of Public Debt in accordance with the provisions of 12 USC 481 and 12 USC 192. The OCC manages risk by diversifying its portfolio across maturities within established parameters. Diversifying maturities of the individual securities is meant to help manage the inherent risk of interest-rate fluctuations.

The OCC's investment portfolio is composed of overnight and longer-term securities. The portion of the portfolio comprising longer-term (core) investments as of September 30, 2012, and September 30, 2011, was $846.5 million, or 62.3 percent, and $645.4 million, or 55.1 percent, respectively. Because of the increase in core investments, the weighted average maturity of the portfolio rose to 2.5 years as of September 30, 2012, compared with 1.6 years as of September 30, 2011. The portfolio earned an annual yield for FY 2012 of 1.9 percent, compared with 2.3 percent in FY 2011.

The OCC calculates annual portfolio yield by dividing the total interest earned during the year by the average ending monthly book value of investments.

Liabilities

The OCC's liabilities represent the resources due to others or held for future recognition and are composed largely of deferred revenue, accrued liabilities, and accounts payable. Deferred revenue represents the unearned portion of semiannual assessments that have been collected but not earned.

As of September 30, 2012, total liabilities were $446.0 million, a net increase of $15.2 million, or 3.5 percent, over total liabilities of $430.8 million on September 30, 2011. The increase of $5.8 million, or 2.5 percent, in deferred revenue was a result of greater assessment collections during FY 2012, the majority of which are attributable to assessments collected from federal savings associations that the OCC supervises. The majority of the increase of $11.1 million, or 8.3 percent, in accounts payable and accrued liabilities was primarily the result of additional accruals related to the leasehold improvement project for the OCC's new headquarters building.

Figure 7 illustrates the OCC's composition of liabilities for FY 2012 and FY 2011.

Figure 7: Composition of Liabilities (in Millions)

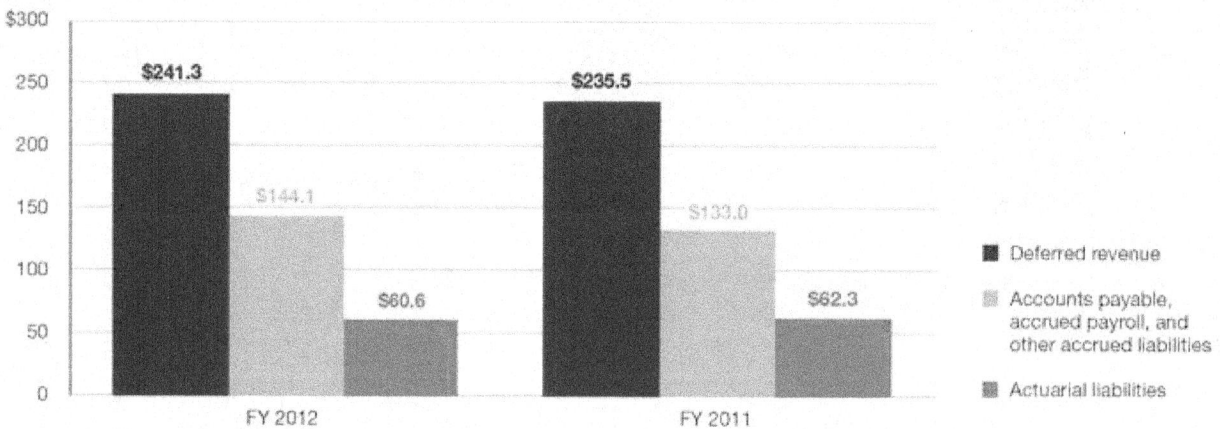

Source: OCC financial system data.

Net Position

The OCC's net position of $1,073.5 million as of September 30, 2012, and $1,095.8 million as of September 30, 2011, represents the cumulative net excess of the OCC's revenues over the cost of operations. The net position is presented on both the Balance Sheets and the Statements of Changes in Net Position.

The OCC reserves a significant portion of the net position to supplement resources made available to fund the OCC's annual budget and to cover foreseeable but rare events or new requirements and opportunities. The OCC also sets aside funds for ongoing operations to cover undelivered orders, the consumption of assets, and capital investments.

Figure 8 shows the OCC's composition of net position for FY 2012 and FY 2011.

Reserves

The establishment of financial reserves is integral to the effective stewardship of the OCC's resources, particularly because the agency does not receive congressional appropriations. The contingency reserve is available to reduce the impact on the OCC's operations of significant revenue fluctuations, of unanticipated expenses resulting from foreseeable but rare events beyond the OCC's control, or of new requirements and opportunities. Examples of such events might include a major change in the federal banking system, a natural disaster that affects one of the OCC's facilities, or significant impairment of the agency's physical infrastructure that interferes with the OCC's ability to accomplish its mission.

These reserves also allow the OCC to fund special onetime needs, such as the funding of the Pentegra Defined Benefit Plan liability assumed from the OTS

Figure 8: Composition of Net Position (in Millions)

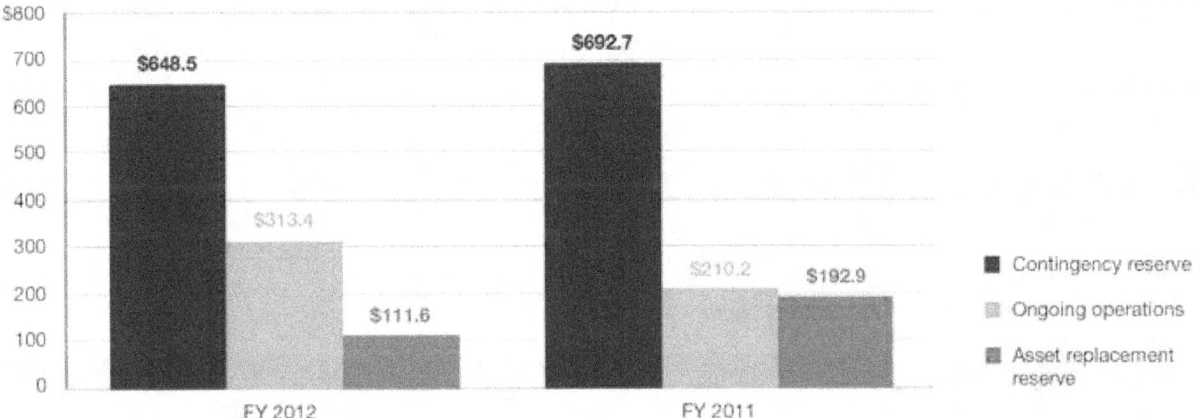

Source: OCC financial system data.

in FY 2011 and those that arose from the regulatory restructuring required by Dodd–Frank.

The asset replacement reserve is for the replacement of information technology investments, leasehold improvements, and furniture replacement for future years. In FY 2012, the asset replacement reserve was used to pay for leasehold improvements and relocation costs as part of the OCC's efforts to consolidate several office locations in Washington, D.C., into one headquarters building.

Revenues

The OCC's operations are funded primarily by assessments collected from national banks and federal savings associations, from interest received on investments in U.S. Treasury securities, and from the rent that the CFPB pays the OCC for leasing office space. The OCC, in accordance with 12 USC 482, establishes budget authority for a given fiscal year. The total budget authority available for use by the OCC in FY 2012 was $1,226.1 million, which represents an increase of $349.6 million, or 39.9 percent, over the $876.5 million budget in FY 2011. The FY 2012 budget increase reflects a full year of operating costs as a combined entity, which includes the staff that transferred from the OTS.

Total FY 2012 revenue of $999.7 million reflects a $156.5 million, or 18.6 percent, increase over

FY 2011 revenues of $843.2 million. The majority of the increase, which was only slightly offset by minor decreases in other revenues, can be attributed to the assessments received from federal savings associations that were not under OCC supervision as of June 30, 2011. Total assets under OCC supervision rose, as of June 30, 2012, to $10.0 trillion, up 13.6 percent from $8.8 trillion a year earlier. Correspondingly, the costs of supervising national banks and federal savings associations have risen because of the increasing size and complexity of their assets. Of this total, $8.0 trillion, or 79.9 percent, is attributable to large national banks. Midsize and community banks' share is $931.0 billion, or 9.3 percent, followed by federal branches at $280.0 billion, or 2.8 percent. Finally, the federal savings association assets totaled $803.1 billion, or 8.0 percent, as of June 30, 2012.

Interest revenue totaled $19.7 million in FY 2012, an increase of $0.3 million, or 1.5 percent, over interest revenue of $19.4 million reported in FY 2011. Other income is composed of revenue received from reimbursable activities with federal entities and the rental revenue the OCC receives from the CFPB, which totaled $3.5 million in FY 2012 (see Note 6).

Figure 9 depicts the components of total revenue for FY 2012 and FY 2011.

Figure 9: Components of Total Revenue (in Millions)

	FY 2012	FY 2011	Change ($)	Change (%)
Assessments	$ 963.6	$ 814.6	$ 149.0	18.3%
Interest and other income	36.1	28.6	7.5	26.2%
Total revenue	$ 999.7	$ 843.2	$ 156.5	18.6%

Source: OCC financial system data.

Cost of Operations

The OCC's net cost of operations is reported on the Statements of Net Cost and the Statements of Changes in Net Position. The OCC uses an activity-based time reporting system to allocate costs among the agency's programs. Costs are further divided into those resulting from transactions between the OCC and other federal entities (intragovernmental) and those between the OCC and nonfederal entities (with the public). The Statements of Net Cost present the full cost of operating the OCC's three major programs—supervise, regulate, and charter national banks and federal savings associations. For FY 2011, the costs associated with operating these programs for federal savings associations are included beginning July 21, 2011.

Figure 10 illustrates the breakdown of costs of operations by major program for FY 2012 and FY 2011.

The full cost presented in the Statements of Net Cost includes costs contributed by the Office of Personnel Management (OPM) on behalf of the OCC to cover the cost of the Federal Employees Retirement System (FERS) and Civil Service Retirement System (CSRS) retirement plans and the Federal Employees Health Benefits (FEHB) and Federal Employees' Group Life Insurance (FEGLI) plans, totaling $32.3 million in FY 2012 and $33.7 million in FY 2011. Total program costs for FY 2012 of $1,049.6 million reflect an increase of $211.9 million, or 25.3 percent, from $837.7 million in FY 2011. The change was due primarily to increased staffing directly related to OTS employees transferred to the OCC. Additional contributing factors included increases to contractual services for systems maintenance and rent.

Budgetary Resources

The Statements of Budgetary Resources, found on page 45, provide information about how budgetary resources were made available to the OCC for the year and present the status of these resources and the net outlay of budgetary resources at the end of the year. The OCC executed $1,140.1 million, or 93.0 percent, of the FY 2012 budget of $1,226.1 million.

Figure 10: Costs of Operations by Major Program (in Millions)

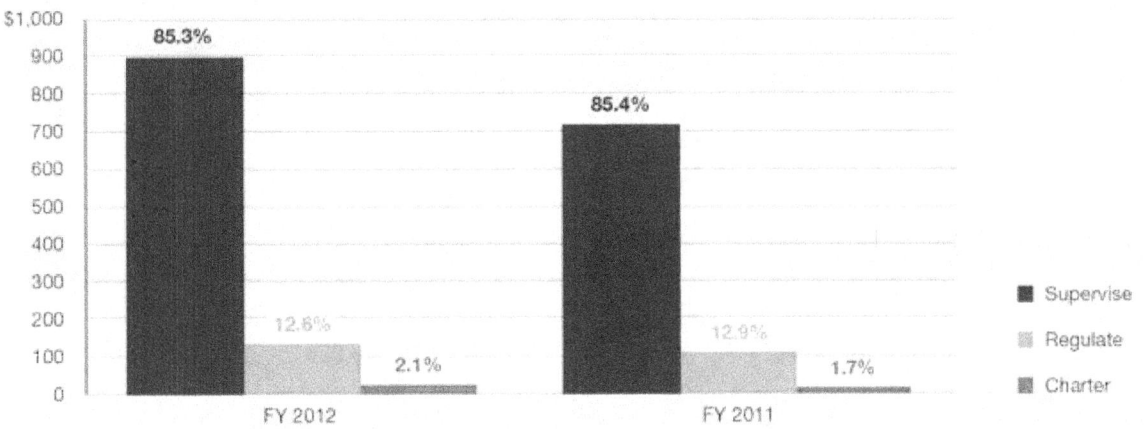

Source: OCC financial system data.

Office of the Comptroller of the Currency
Balance Sheets
As of September 30, 2012 and 2011
(in Thousands)

		2012		2011
Assets				
Intragovernmental:				
Fund balance with Treasury (Note 2)	$	8,814	$	237,036
Investments and related interest (Note 3)		1,380,006		1,188,159
Accounts receivable (Note 4)		2,035		3,931
Other assets		558		316
Total intragovernmental		1,391,413		1,429,442
Accounts receivable, net (Note 4)		471		542
Property and equipment, net (Note 5)		127,568		96,617
Other assets		15		24
Total assets	$	1,519,467	$	1,526,625
Liabilities				
Intragovernmental:				
Accounts payable and other accrued liabilities	$	7,913	$	3,300
Total intragovernmental		7,913		3,300
Accounts payable		3,571		8,056
Accrued payroll and benefits		40,930		43,811
Accrued annual leave		46,366		47,630
Other accrued liabilities		45,271		30,249
Deferred revenue		241,348		235,514
Other actuarial liabilities (Note 8)		60,611		62,272
Total liabilities		446,010		430,832
Net position (Note 9)		1,073,457		1,095,793
Total liabilities and net position	$	1,519,467	$	1,526,625

The accompanying notes are an integral part of these financial statements.

Office of the Comptroller of the Currency
Statements of Net Cost
For the Years Ended September 30, 2012 and 2011
(in Thousands)

	2012	2011
Program costs		
Supervise		
Intragovernmental	$ 115,089	$ 103,977
With the public	780,112	611,387
Subtotal – supervise	$ 895,201	$ 715,364
Regulate		
Intragovernmental	$ 17,722	$ 16,003
With the public	114,612	91,977
Subtotal – regulate	$ 132,334	$ 107,980
Charter		
Intragovernmental	$ 2,995	$ 2,212
With the public	19,071	12,148
Subtotal – charter	$ 22,066	$ 14,360
Total program costs	$ 1,049,601	$ 837,704
Less: earned revenues not attributed to programs	(999,727)	(843,203)
Net program costs before gain/loss from changes in assumptions	$ 49,874	$ (5,499)
Actuarial (gain)/loss (Note 8)	4,335	(196)
Net cost of operations (Note 10)	$ 54,209	$ (5,695)

The accompanying notes are an integral part of these financial statements.

Office of the Comptroller of the Currency
Statements of Changes in Net Position
For the Years Ended September 30, 2012 and 2011
(in Thousands)

	2012	2011
Beginning balances	$ 1,095,793	$ 785,454
Budgetary financing sources:		
Transfer-in without reimbursement	0	259,222
Other financing sources:		
Transfer-in/out without reimbursement	(434)	11,675
Imputed financing (Note 11)	32,307	33,747
Net cost of operations	(54,209)	5,695
Net change	(22,336)	310,339
Ending balances	$ 1,073,457	$ 1,095,793

The accompanying notes are an integral part of these financial statements.

Office of the Comptroller of the Currency
Statements of Budgetary Resources
For the Years Ended September 30, 2012 and 2011

(in Thousands)

		2012		2011
Budgetary resources:				
Unobligated balance brought forward, October 1	$	1,162,804	$	847,259
Adjustment to unobligated balance brought forward, October 1		0		0
Unobligated balance from prior year budget authority, net		1,162,804		847,259
Balance transfers		0		245,034
Spending authority from offsetting collections		1,001,516		895,505
Total budgetary resources	$	**2,164,320**	$	**1,987,798**
Status of budgetary resources:				
Obligations incurred	$	1,077,171	$	824,994
Exempt from apportionment		1,087,149		1,162,804
Unapportioned		0		0
Total unobligated balance, end of year		1,087,149		1,162,804
Total budgetary resources	$	**2,164,320**	$	**1,987,798**
Change in obligated balance:				
Unpaid obligation balance brought forward, October 1	$	251,164	$	184,501
Obligations incurred		1,077,171		824,993
Outlay (gross)		(1,043,822)		(797,892)
Actual transfers, unpaid obligations (net)		0		39,562
Unpaid obligation, end of year		284,513		251,164
Uncollected payment, federal source brought forward, October 1		(7,493)		(3,579)
Change in uncollected payment, federal source		1,515		(3,914)
Uncollected payment, federal source, end of year		(5,978)		(7,493)
Memorandum (non-add) entries				
Obligated balance, start of year	$	243,671	$	180,922
Obligated balance, end of year	$	278,535	$	243,671
Budget authority and outlays, net:				
Budget authority, gross	$	1,001,516	$	895,505
Actual offsetting collections		(1,003,031)		(891,591)
Change in uncollected payment from federal source		1,515		(3,914)
Budget authority, net		0		0
Outlay, gross		1,043,822		797,892
Actual offsetting collections		(1,003,031)		(891,591)
Agency outlay, net	$	**40,791**	$	**(93,699)**

The accompanying notes are an integral part of these financial statements.

Note 1—Significant Accounting Policies

Reporting Entity

The OCC was created as a bureau within the Treasury Department by an act of Congress in 1863. The mission of the OCC was to establish and regulate a system of federally chartered national banks. The National Currency Act of 1863, rewritten and reenacted as the National Bank Act of 1864, authorized the OCC to supervise national banks and to regulate the lending and investment activities of federally chartered institutions. With the passage of Dodd–Frank on July 21, 2010, the OCC also oversees federally chartered savings associations.

The financial statements report on the OCC's three major programs: supervise, regulate, and charter national banks and federal savings associations. The OCC's major programs support the agency's overall mission by ensuring a safe and sound system of national banks and federal savings associations; promoting equal access to financial services and fair treatment of bank customers; maintaining a flexible legal and regulatory framework that enables a strong, competitive system of banks; and having a competent, highly motivated, and diverse workforce.

Basis of Accounting and Presentation

The OCC's financial statements are prepared from the agency's accounting records in conformity with GAAP as set forth by the Federal Accounting Standards Advisory Board (FASAB). The OCC's financial statements are presented in accordance with the form and content guidelines established by the OMB in Circular No. A-136, "Financial Reporting Requirements."

In addition, the OCC applies financial accounting and reporting standards issued by the Financial Accounting Standards Board (FASB) only as outlined in Statement of Federal Financial Accounting Standards (SFFAS) 34, "The Hierarchy of Generally Accepted Accounting Principles," including the "Application of Standards Issued by the Financial Accounting Standards Board."

The OCC's financial statements consist of Balance Sheets, Statements of Net Cost, Statements of Changes in Net Position, and Statements of Budgetary

Resources. The OCC chose early adoption for the formatting changes of the Statements of Budgetary Resources, which are required in FY 2013 by Circular No. A-136. The OCC presents its financial statements on a comparative basis, providing information for FY 2012 and FY 2011. The accompanying financial statements and notes present the operations of the OCC, which include the functions transferred from the OTS in FY 2011.

The financial statements reflect both the accrual and budgetary bases of accounting. Under the accrual basis of accounting, revenues are recognized when earned, and expenses are recognized when a liability is incurred, without regard to cash receipt or payment. The budgetary method recognizes the obligation of funds according to legal requirements, which in many cases is recorded before the occurrence of an accrual-based transaction. Budgetary accounting is essential for compliance with legal constraints and controls over the use of federal funds.

In accordance with GAAP, the preparation of financial statements requires management to make estimates and assumptions that affect the reported amounts of assets and liabilities, the disclosure of contingent assets and liabilities at the date of the financial statements, and the reported amounts of revenue and expense during the reporting period. Such estimates and assumptions could change in the future as more information becomes known, which could affect the amounts reported and disclosed herein.

Throughout these financial statements, assets, liabilities, earned revenues, and costs have been classified according to the entity responsible for these transactions. Intragovernmental earned revenues are collections or accruals of revenue from other federal entities, and intragovernmental costs are payments or accruals of expenditures to other federal entities. The Statements of Budgetary Resources for FY 2011 has been reclassified to make it comparable to the FY 2012 presentation.

Revenues and Other Financing Sources

The OCC derives its revenue primarily from assessments and fees paid by national banks and federal savings associations, and from income on investments in non-marketable U.S. Treasury securities. The OCC does not receive congressional appropriations to fund any of the agency's operations. Therefore, the OCC has no unexpended appropriations.

By federal statute 12 USC 481, the OCC's funds are maintained in a U.S. government trust revolving fund. The funds remain available to cover the annual costs of the OCC's operations in accordance with policies established by the Comptroller of the Currency. As part of the OTS integration in FY 2011, a second fund symbol was temporarily established. This fund symbol was closed at the end of FY 2012.

Earmarked Funds

Earmarked funds are financed by specifically identified revenues, often supplemented by other financing sources, which remain available over time. These specifically identified revenues and other financing sources are required by statute to be used for designated activities, benefits, or purposes, and must be accounted for separately from the government's general revenues. In accordance with FASAB SFFAS No. 27, "Identifying and Reporting Earmarked Funds," all of the OCC's revenue meets this criterion and constitutes an earmarked fund.

Fund Balance With Treasury

The Treasury Department processes the OCC's cash receipts and disbursements. The OCC's Statements of Budgetary Resources reflect the status of the agency's FBWT (see Note 2).

Investments

It is the OCC's policy to invest available funds in accordance with the provisions of 12 USC 481 and 12 USC 192. The OCC invests available funds in non-marketable U.S. Treasury securities, which may include overnight securities, bills, notes, and bonds. The OCC does not invest funds with state or national banks. The OCC has the positive intent and ability to hold all U.S. Treasury securities to maturity in accordance with FASB Accounting Standards Codification (ASC) Topic 320, "Investments—Debt and Equity Securities" (see Note 3).

Accounts Receivable

In accordance with SFFAS No. 1, "Accounting for Selected Assets and Liabilities," the OCC updates the "allowance for loss on accounts receivable" account annually or as needed to reflect the most current estimate of accounts that are likely to be uncollectible. Accounts receivable from the public are reduced by an allowance for loss on doubtful accounts (see Note 4).

Property and Equipment

Property and equipment as well as internal-use software are accounted for in accordance with SFFAS No. 6, "Accounting for Property, Plant, and Equipment," and SFFAS No. 10, "Accounting for Internal Use Software."

Property and equipment purchases and additions are stated at cost. The OCC expenses purchases that do not meet the capitalization criteria, such as normal repairs and maintenance, when received or incurred.

In addition, property and equipment are depreciated or amortized, as applicable, over the estimated useful lives using the straight-line method and are removed from the OCC's asset accounts in the period of disposal, retirement, or removal from service. Any difference between the book value of the property and equipment and amounts realized is recognized as a gain or loss in the same period that the asset is removed (see Note 5).

Liabilities

The OCC records liabilities for amounts that are likely to be paid as a result of events that have occurred as of the relevant Balance Sheet dates. The OCC's liabilities consist of routine operating accounts payable, accrued payroll and benefits, and deferred revenue. The OCC's liabilities represent the amounts owed or accrued under contractual or other arrangements governing the transactions, including operating expenses incurred but not paid. The OCC accounts for liabilities in accordance with SFFAS No. 5, "Accounting for Liabilities of the Federal Government."

Accounts Payable

Payments are made in a timely manner in accordance with the Prompt Payment Act. Interest penalties are paid when payments are late. Discounts are taken when cost effective and when the invoices are paid within the discount period.

Accrued Annual Leave

In accordance with SFFAS No. 5, annual leave is accrued and funded by the OCC as it is earned, and the accrual is reduced as leave is taken or paid. Each year, the balance in the accrued annual leave account is adjusted to reflect actual leave balances with current pay rates. Sick leave and other types of leave are expensed as incurred.

Deferred Revenue

The OCC's activities are primarily financed by assessments on assets held by national banks, federal savings associations, and the federal branches of foreign banks. These assessments are due March 31 and September 30 of each year, based on their asset balances as of December 31 and June 30, respectively. Assessments are paid mid-cycle and are recognized as earned revenue on a straight-line basis. The unearned portions of collected assessments are classified as deferred revenue.

Employment Benefits

Retirement Plans

All of the OCC's employees participate in one of three retirement systems—the CSRS, FERS, or the Pentegra DB Plan. The CSRS and FERS are administered by OPM. Pursuant to the enactment of Public Law 99-335, which established FERS, most OCC employees hired after December 31, 1983, are automatically covered by FERS and Social Security. Employees hired before January 1, 1984, are covered by the CSRS, with the exception of those who, during the election period, joined FERS.

The OCC does not report CSRS or FERS assets or accumulated plan benefits that may be applicable to its employees in its financial statements; OPM reports them. Although the OCC reports no liability for future payments to employees under these programs, the federal government is liable for future payments to employees through the various agencies administering these programs.

The OCC assumed the role of benefit administrator for the Pentegra DB Plan in FY 2011. The Pentegra DB Plan covers some of the transferred OTS employees and is closed to new entrants. The OCC is committed to adhering to sound financial policies and management oversight of the plan to ensure its sustainability for current and future retirees.

Thrift Savings Plan and OCC 401(k) Plan

The OCC's employees are eligible to participate in the federal Thrift Savings Plan. OCC employees also can elect to contribute a portion of their base pay to the OCC-sponsored 401(k) plan, subject to Internal Revenue Service regulations that apply to employee contributions in both the federal Thrift Savings Plan and the OCC-sponsored 401(k) plan.

As required by law, for OTS employees transferred to the OCC, the OCC continues to offer a separate 401(k) plan. The amount of each participant's matching contribution is based on the applicable retirement system under which each participant is covered.

Federal Employees Health Benefits and Federal Employees' Group Life Insurance

Employees and retirees of the OCC are eligible to participate in the FEHB and FEGLI plans administered by OPM that involve a cost sharing of biweekly coverage premiums by employee and employer. The OCC does not fund post-retirement benefits for these programs. Instead, the OCC's financial statements recognize an imputed financing source and corresponding expense that represent the OCC's share of the cost to the federal government of providing these benefits to all eligible OCC employees.

Post-Retirement Life Insurance Benefit Plan

The OCC sponsors a life insurance benefit plan for current and retired employees. On July 29, 2012, former OTS employees were converted to the OCC life insurance benefit plan. This plan is a defined benefit plan for which the benefit is earned over the period from the employee's date of hire to the date on which the employee is assumed to retire. The valuation of the plan is conducted in accordance with generally accepted actuarial principles and practices, including the applicable Actuarial Standards of Practice as issued by the Actuarial Standards Board. Specifically, the OCC uses the actuarial cost method as outlined in FASB ASC Topic 715, "Compensation—Retirement Benefits," to determine costs for its retirement plans. Gains or losses owing to changes in actuarial assumptions are amortized over the service life of the plan. The actuarial assumptions and methods used in calculating actuarial amounts comply with the requirements for post-retirement benefits other than pensions as set forth in FASB ASC Topic 715 and for health benefit plans as set forth in American Institute of Certified Public Accountants Statement of Position 92-6.

In addition, for the one-year period following the transfer date (through July 21, 2012), the OCC continued to administer a separate life insurance plan for those OTS employees transferred to the OCC who met eligibility requirements (see Note 8).

Custodial Revenues and Collections

Non-entity receivables, liabilities, and revenue are recorded as custodial activity and include amounts collected for fines, CMPs, and related interest assessments. Revenues are recognized as cash collected that are transferred to the General Fund of the U.S. Treasury at the end of the fiscal year.

Note 2—Fund Balance With Treasury

The status of the FBWT represents the budgetary resources that support the FBWT and is a reconciliation between budgetary and proprietary accounts. The OCC's FBWT comprises two separate U.S. Treasury fund symbols. The first is designated as a trust fund established by 12 USC 481 that governs the collection and use of assessments and other funds

by the OCC. The second fund symbol is designated as a revolving fund and was established to allow for the transfer of OTS funds to the OCC on July 21, 2011. All transferred funds have been expended, and as of September 30, 2012, the revolving fund was closed.

The OCC's FBWT consists of unobligated and obligated balances that reflect the budgetary authority remaining for disbursement against current or future obligations. The unobligated balance represents the cumulative amount of budgetary authority that has not been set aside to cover outstanding obligations and is classified as available for future OCC use without further congressional action. The obligated balance not yet disbursed represents funds that have been obligated for goods that have not been received or services that have not been performed. It also represents goods and services that have been delivered or received but for which payment has not been made. The nonbudgetary FBWT account represents adjustments to budgetary accounts that do not affect the FBWT. The OCC's balance represents investment accounts that reduce the status of the FBWT.

As of September 30, 2012, there were no unreconciled differences between U.S. Treasury records and balances reported on the OCC's general ledger.

The figure below depicts the OCC's FBWT amounts for FY 2012 and FY 2011.

Fund Balance With Treasury (in Thousands)

	FY 2012		FY 2011	
Fund balance				
Trust fund	$	8,814	$	10,623
Revolving fund	$	0	$	226,413
Total fund balance	$	**8,814**	$	**237,036**
Status of fund balance with Treasury				
Unobligated balance—available	$	1,087,149	$	1,162,804
Obligated balance not yet disbursed		278,535		243,671
Non-budgetary fund balance with Treasury		(1,356,870)		(1,169,439)
Total	$	**8,814**	$	**237,036**

Note 3—Investments and Related Interest

The OCC's investments are stated at amortized cost and the related accrued interest. Premiums and discounts are amortized over the term of the investment using the effective interest method. The fair market value of investment securities was $1,416.3 million on September 30, 2012, and $1,223.5 million on September 30, 2011. The overall portfolio earned an annual yield of 1.9 percent for FY 2012 and 2.3 percent for FY 2011.

The yield-to-maturity on the non-overnight portion of the OCC's investment portfolio ranged from 0.2 percent to 4.5 percent in FY 2012 and from 0.9 percent to 4.5 percent in FY 2011.

FY 2012 Investments and Related Interest (in Thousands)

	Cost	Amortization method	Amortized (premium) discount	Investments, net	Market value disclosure
Intragovernmental securities:					
Non-marketable market-based	$ 1,386,220	Effective interest	$ (10,158)	$ 1,376,062	$ 1,416,347
Accrued interest	3,944		0	3,944	3,944
Total intragovernmental investments	$ 1,390,164		$ (10,158)	$ 1,380,006	$ 1,420,291

FY 2011 Investments and Related Interest (in Thousands)

	Cost	Amortization method	Amortized (premium) discount	Investments, net	Market value disclosure
Intragovernmental securities:					
Non-marketable market-based	$ 1,192,820	Effective interest	$ (8,224)	$ 1,184,596	$ 1,223,491
Accrued interest	3,563		0	3,563	3,563
Total intragovernmental investments	$ 1,196,383		$ (8,224)	$ 1,188,159	$ 1,227,054

Note 4—Accounts Receivable

As presented in the OCC's Balance Sheets, accounts receivable represent monies due from the public for services and goods provided that are retained by the OCC upon collection. The amounts shown for federal receivables represent pension sharing costs for OTS employees transferred to other federal agencies rather than to the OCC. Also included are CMP amounts assessed against people, national banks, or federal savings associations for violations of law, regulation, and orders; unsafe or unsound practices; and breaches of fiduciary duty. Because CMPs are not debts due the OCC, the amount outstanding does not enter into the calculation for the allowance for uncollectible accounts. The OCC has recognized $55.4 million and $41.6 million in CMP non-entity revenue as of September 30, 2012, and 2011, respectively.

FY 2012 Accounts Receivable (in Thousands)

	Gross		Allowance for uncollectible accounts		Account receivable, net	
Federal receivables	$	2,035	$	0	$	2,035
Civil money penalty receivables		417		0		417
Nonfederal receivables		79		(25)		54
Total accounts receivable	$	2,531	$	(25)	$	2,506

FY 2011 Accounts Receivable (in Thousands)

	Gross		Allowance for uncollectible accounts		Account receivable, net	
Federal receivables	$	3,931	$	0	$	3,931
Civil money penalty receivables		486		0		486
Nonfederal receivables		81		(25)		56
Total accounts receivable	$	4,498	$	(25)	$	4,473

Note 5—Property and Equipment, Net

Property and equipment purchased at a cost greater than or equal to the noted thresholds below with useful lives of three years or more are capitalized at cost and depreciated or amortized, as applicable. Depreciation is expensed on a straight-line basis over the estimated useful life of the asset with the exception of leasehold improvements. Leasehold improvements are amortized on a straight-line basis over the lesser of the terms of the related leases or the estimated useful lives. Land, leasehold improvements in development, and internal-use software in development are not depreciated. Major alterations and renovations, including leasehold and land improvements, are capitalized, while maintenance and repair costs are charged to expenses as incurred. All other property and equipment are depreciated or amortized, as applicable, on a straight-line basis over the estimated useful lives.

For FY 2012 and FY 2011, the OCC reported $2.2 million and $1.9 million, respectively, of fully depreciated assets removed from service, which included a $0.4 million transfer of assets to the CFPB. In FY 2012 and FY 2011, there were no gains or losses on asset disposal. The figures below summarize property and equipment balances as of September 30, 2012, and 2011.

FY 2012 and FY 2011 assets include the land and a building owned by the OTS that were transferred to the OCC on July 21, 2011. The building is a rental-income property that the OCC uses to supplement its operating budget (see Note 6).

FY 2012 Property and Equipment, Net (in Thousands)

Class of assets	Capitalization threshold	Useful life (in years)	Cost	Accumulated depreciation/ amortization	Net book value
Land	NA	NA	$ 7,101	$ 0	$ 7,101
Building	50	50	49,188	(32,865)	16,323
Leasehold improvements	50	5-20	103,553	(58,049)	45,504
Equipment	50	3-10	40,775	(26,882)	13,893
Internal-use software	500	5	80,546	(65,275)	15,271
Internal-use software—development	500	NA	18,627	0	18,627
Leasehold improvements—development	50	NA	10,849	0	10,849
Total			$ 310,639	$ (183,071)	$ 127,568

FY 2011 Property and Equipment, Net (in Thousands)

Class of assets	Capitalization threshold	Useful life (in years)	Cost	Accumulated depreciation/ amortization	Net book value
Land	NA	NA	$ 7,101	$ 0	$ 7,101
Building	50	50	49,188	(31,812)	17,376
Leasehold improvements	50	5-20	78,766	(48,536)	30,230
Equipment	50	3-10	30,918	(24,170)	6,748
Internal-use software	500	5	69,025	(57,797)	11,228
Internal-use software—development	500	NA	19,990	0	19,990
Leasehold improvements—development	50	NA	3,944	0	3,944
Total			$ 258,932	$ (162,315)	$ 96,617

Note: NA means not applicable.

Note 6—Rental Income

In FY 2012, the OCC entered into a 20-year occupancy agreement with the CFPB for a portion of the former OTS headquarters building transferred to the OCC in FY 2011. After the transfer date, the OCC also assumed ownership from the OTS of its existing non-cancellable operating leases for additional space in that building and began receiving rental income from building tenants. These leases expire at various dates through 2021, and some provide renewal options. The leases provide for annual base rent and additional rents for building operating expenses. Some leases also provide for fixed future increases in rents over the term of the lease.

The future minimum rentals to be received through FY 2018 and thereafter, not including renewals, are shown below.

FY 2012 Future Rental Income (in Thousands)

Year	Amount
2013	$ 12,058
2014	12,313
2015	12,287
2016	12,534
2017	12,678
2018 and beyond	210,394
Total	$ 272,264

FY 2011 Future Rental Income (in Thousands)

Year	Amount
2012	$ 2,468
2013	647
2014	599
2015	374
2016	305
2017 and beyond	1,141
Total	$ 5,534

Note 7—Leases

The OCC leases equipment and office space for its Headquarters operations in Washington, D.C., and for district and field operations. During FY 2012, the OCC entered into six new lease occupancy agreements that ranged between 54 and 120 months. All of the OCC's leases are treated as operating leases. All annual lease costs under the operating leases are included in the Statements of Net Cost.

The future minimum lease payments to be made through FY 2018 and thereafter, not including renewals, are shown below.

FY 2012 Future Lease Payments (in Thousands)

Year	Amount
2013	$ 68,431
2014	54,039
2015	49,694
2016	47,344
2017	48,914
2018 and beyond	378,267
Total	$ 646,689

FY 2011 Future Lease Payments (in Thousands)

Year	Amount
2012	$ 45,569
2013	59,915
2014	48,826
2015	45,078
2016	45,657
2017 and beyond	420,088
Total	$ 665,133

Note 8—Other Actuarial Liabilities

The OCC's other actuarial liabilities are reported on the Balance Sheets and include the following components.

Actuarial Liabilities Category (in Thousands)

Component	FY 2012		FY 2011	
Post-retirement life insurance benefits	$	54,101	$	47,732
Federal Employees' Compensation Act		5,825		5,513
Pentegra Defined Benefit Plan		685		9,027
Total actuarial liabilities	$	60,611	$	62,272

Post-Retirement Life Insurance Benefits

The OCC sponsors a life insurance benefit plan for current and retired employees. In addition, for one year after the transfer date (through July 21, 2012), the OCC administered a separate life insurance plan for former OTS employees who met eligibility requirements. Transferred OTS plan participants were converted to the OCC-sponsored plan on July 29, 2012. The weighted-average discount rate used in determining the accumulated post-retirement benefit obligation was 4.25 percent and 4.75 percent for FY 2012 and FY 2011, respectively. Gains or losses owing to changes in actuarial assumptions are amortized over the service life of the plan.

Net periodic post-retirement benefit costs for life insurance provisions under the plans include the components shown on this page. The total benefit expenses are recognized as program costs in the Statements of Net Cost. Any gains or losses from changes in long-term assumptions used to measure liabilities for post-retirement life insurance benefits are displayed separately on the Statements of Net Cost, as required.

The following table presents a reconciliation of the beginning and ending post-retirement life insurance liability and provides material components of the related expenses.

Reconciliation of Beginning and Ending Post-Retirement Liability and the Related Expense (in Thousands)

Change in actuarial and accrued benefits	FY 2012		FY 2011	
Actuarial post-retirement liability beginning balance	$	47,732	$	45,472
Actuarial expense				
Normal cost		1,153		1,374
Interest on the liability balance		2,280		2,385
Actuarial (gain)/loss				
From experience		(422)		495
From assumption changes		4,757		(691)
Prior service costs		0		80
Total expense		7,768		3,643
Less amounts paid		(1,399)		(1,383)
Actuarial post-retirement liability ending balance	$	54,101	$	47,732

Federal Employees' Compensation Act

The Federal Employees' Compensation Act provides income and medical cost protection to cover federal civilian employees injured on the job, employees who have incurred a work-related occupational disease, and beneficiaries of employees whose death is attributable to a job-related injury or occupational disease. Claims incurred for benefits for OCC employees covered under the Federal Employees' Compensation Act are administered by the U.S. Department of Labor and later billed to the OCC. The FY 2012 and FY 2011 present values of these estimated outflows are calculated using a discount rate of 2.3 percent in the first year and 3.1 percent in subsequent years, and 3.5 percent in the first year and 4.0 percent in subsequent years, respectively.

Pentegra Defined Benefit Plan

In accordance with the provisions of Dodd–Frank, in FY 2011 the OCC assumed the role of benefit administrator for a legacy retirement system—the Pentegra DB Plan. The Pentegra DB Plan is a defined benefit plan that the OTS assumed from its predecessor agency when the OTS was created in 1989.
The Pentegra DB Plan is a system in which all costs are paid by the employer into one general account. At retirement, employees may either receive a lump sum payment or opt for an annuity/lump sum split.

As a result of Dodd–Frank, FY 2012 is the first full year disclosed for the Pentegra DB Plan, which ran

from July 1, 2011, through June 30, 2012. Total expenses recognized were $2.7 million during FY 2012 and $9.0 million during FY 2011. For actuarial purposes, the liability was fully funded at September 30, 2012, and is therefore not reflected in the FY 2012 Balance Sheets. As of September 30, 2011, the liability was underfunded by $86.2 million. Total plan assets as of July 1, 2012, were $562.1 million.

The following table presents a reconciliation of the beginning and ending Pentegra DB Plan liability and provides material components of the related expenses.

Reconciliation of Beginning and Ending Pentegra DB Plan Liability and the Related Expense (in Thousands)

Change in actuarial and accrued benefits	FY 2012
Actuarial liability beginning balance	$ 534,637
Actuarial expense	
Normal cost	18,406
Interest on the liability balance	11,186
Actuarial (gain)/loss	
From experience	(15,846)
From assumption changes	(41,390)
Prior service costs	0
Total expense	(27,644)
Less amounts paid	(23,258)
Actuarial liability ending balance	**$ 483,735**

Note 9—Net Position

Net position represents the net result of operations since inception and includes cumulative amounts related to investments in capitalized assets held by the OCC. The OCC sets aside a portion of its net position as contingency and asset replacement reserves for use at the Comptroller's discretion. In addition, funds are set aside to cover the cost of ongoing operations.

The contingency reserve supports the OCC's ability to accomplish its mission by being available to reduce the impact on the OCC's operations from significant revenue fluctuations, such as those resulting from a major change in the federal banking system. Also covered are unanticipated expenses resulting from foreseeable but rare events beyond the OCC's control, including a natural disaster that affects one of the

OCC's facilities and significant impairment of the agency's physical infrastructure.

The asset replacement reserve funds the replacement of information technology investments, leasehold improvements, and furniture replacements for future years. The target level for the replacement reserve is established annually based on the gross value of existing property and equipment plus a growth-rate factor and a margin for market cost adjustments.

The figure below reflects balances for FY 2012 and FY 2011. In FY 2012, the asset replacement reserve was used to consolidate several office locations in Washington, D.C., into one headquarters building. In addition, in FY 2012, the contingency reserve was used for onetime costs associated with the OTS integration.

Net Position Availability (in Thousands)

Component	FY 2012	FY 2011
Contingency reserve	$ 648,463	$ 692,690
Asset replacement reserve	111,600	192,900
Set aside for ongoing operations:		
Undelivered orders	122,505	64,440
Consumption of assets	147,334	112,114
Capital investments	43,555	33,649
Net position	$ 1,073,457	$ 1,095,793

Note 10—Net Cost of Operations

The Net Cost of Operations represents the OCC's operating costs deducted from assessments and fees paid by national banks and federal saving associations and other income earned. The operating costs include the gain or loss from actuarial experience and assumption changes per the guidance in

SFFAS No. 33. The imputed financing sources for net cost of operations are reported on the Statements of Changes in Net Position and in Note 12, Reconciliation of Net Cost of Operations to Budget.

The following figure illustrates the OCC's operating expense categories for FY 2012 and FY 2011.

Net Cost of Operations by Expense Category (in Thousands)

	FY 2012	FY 2011
Personnel compensation and benefits	$ 741,516	$ 546,739
Contractual services	124,823	115,912
Rent, communication, and utilities	61,513	50,381
Travel and transportation of persons and things	55,082	51,963
Imputed costs	32,307	33,747
Depreciation	22,554	18,437
Other	16,141	20,329
Total	$ 1,053,936	$ 837,508

Note 11—Imputed Costs and Financing Sources

In accordance with SFFAS No. 5, "Accounting for Liabilities of the Federal Government," federal agencies must recognize the portion of employees' pension and other retirement benefits to be paid by OPM trust funds. These amounts are recorded as imputed costs and imputed financing for other agencies. Annually, OPM provides federal agencies with cost factors for the computation of current year imputed costs. These cost factors are multiplied by the current year salary or number of employees, as applicable, to provide an estimate of the imputed financing that OPM trust funds will provide for each agency.

The imputed costs categories for FY 2012 and FY 2011 are listed in the table below. These imputed costs are included on the Statements of Net Cost. The financing sources absorbed by the OPM are reflected on the Statements of Changes in Net Position and in Note 12, Reconciliation of Net Cost of Operations to Budget.

Note 12—Reconciliation of Net Cost of Operations to Budget

The Reconciliation of Net Cost of Operations to Budget demonstrates the relationship between the OCC's proprietary accounting (net cost of operations) and budgetary accounting (net obligations) information. For FY 2012, the statement on the next page shows a total use of resources to finance activities of $108.0 million. This is a net decrease of $132.6 million from September 30, 2011, when there were excess resources of $25.1 million. This net decrease resulted primarily from a $106.0 million increase in resources available (spending authority from offsetting collections) netted against the increase of $252.2 million in resources used (obligations incurred), and the $1.4 million decrease in imputed financing. The majority of the increase in resources was used to fully fund the Pentegra DB Plan.

Imputed Costs Absorbed by the OPM (in Thousands)

Component	FY 2012		FY 2011	
Retirement	$	14,889	$	16,163
Federal Employees Health Benefits		17,375		17,545
Federal Employees' Group Life Insurance		43		39
Total imputed costs covered by the OPM	$	32,307	$	33,747

Office of the Comptroller of the Currency
Reconciliation of Net Cost of Operations to Budget
For the Years Ended September 30, 2012 and 2011
(in Thousands)

	2012	2011
Resources used to finance activities		
Budgetary resources obligated		
Obligations incurred	$ 1,077,171	$ 824,994
Less: Spending authority from offsetting collections	(1,001,516)	(895,505)
Net obligations	75,655	(70,511)
Other resources		
Transfer-in (out) without reimbursement	(433)	11,675
Imputed financing sources (Note 11)	32,307	33,747
Total resources used to finance activities	**107,529**	**(25,089)**
Resources used to finance items not part of the net cost of operations		
Change in budgetary resources obligated for goods, services, and benefits ordered but not yet provided	(24,170)	10,903
Resources that finance the acquisition of assets	(53,937)	(25,821)
Adjustment to net obligated balance that does not affect net cost of operations	433	(11,675)
Total resources used to finance items not part of the net cost of operations	(77,674)	(26,593)
Total resources used to finance the net cost of operations	**$ 29,855**	**$ (51,682)**
Components of the net cost of operations that will not require or generate resources in the current period		
Components requiring or generating resources in future periods		
Change in deferred revenue	5,834	41,071
Increase in exchange revenue receivable from the public	2	9,478
Total components that will require or generate resources in future periods	5,836	50,549
Components not requiring or generating resources		
Depreciation and amortization	22,554	18,437
Net increase (decrease) in bond premium	(4,036)	1,742
Other	0	(24,741)
Total components that will not require or generate resources	18,518	(4,562)
Total components of net cost of operations that will not require or generate resources in the current period	**24,354**	**45,987**
Net cost of operations	**$ 54,209**	**$ (5,695)**

Note 13—Commitments and Contingencies

The OCC recognizes and discloses contingencies in accordance with SFFAS No. 12, "Recognition of Contingent Liabilities Arising From Litigation." The OCC is party to various administrative proceedings, legal actions, and claims brought against the agency, including threatened or pending litigation involving federal employment claims, some of which may ultimately result in settlements or decisions against the federal government.

As of September 30, 2012, there were four contingencies for litigations involving the OCC where the risk of loss was reasonably possible. For three of these, there was a reasonable possibility that the OCC could incur a loss of $1.5 million, which comprises $600,000 in back pay and $900,000 in compensatory damages. For the fourth contingency, the OCC could incur a loss of up to $675,000.

As of September 30, 2011, the OCC reported $1.5 million for contingencies where the loss was reasonably possible and $191,000 for a contingency where the risk of loss was probable.

Certified Public Accountants
& Consultants

www.gkacpa.com

Independent Auditor's Report on Financial Statements

Inspector General, Department of the Treasury, and
the Comptroller of the Currency:

We have audited the accompanying balance sheets of the Office of the Comptroller of the Currency (OCC) as of September 30, 2012 and 2011, and the related statements of net cost, changes in net position and budgetary resources (hereinafter referred to as "financial statements") for the years then ended. These financial statements are the responsibility of the management of OCC. Our responsibility is to express an opinion on these financial statements based on our audits.

We conducted our audits in accordance with auditing standards generally accepted in the United States of America; the standards applicable to financial audits contained in *Government Auditing Standards*, issued by the Comptroller General of the United States; and applicable provisions of Office of Management and Budget Bulletin No. 07-04, *Audit Requirements for Federal Financial Statements*, as amended. Those standards require that we plan and perform the audits to obtain reasonable assurance about whether the financial statements are free of material misstatement. An audit includes examining, on a test basis, evidence supporting the amounts and disclosures in the financial statements. An audit also includes assessing the accounting principles used and significant estimates made by management, as well as evaluating the overall financial statement presentation. We believe that our audits provide a reasonable basis for our opinion.

In our opinion, the financial statements referred to above present fairly, in all material respects, the financial position of the OCC as of September 30, 2012 and 2011, and its net costs, changes in net position, and budgetary resources for the years then ended in conformity with accounting principles generally accepted in the United States of America.

U.S. generally accepted accounting principles require that the information in Section Five, pages 35 through 41, and pages 69 and 70 be presented to supplement the basic financial statements referred to in the first paragraph of this report. Such information, although not a part of the basic financial statements, is required by the Federal Accounting Standards Advisory Board who considers it to be an essential

1015 18th Street, NW
Suite 200
Washington, DC 20036
Tel: 202-857-1777
Fax: 202-857-1778

part of financial reporting for placing the basic financial statements in an appropriate operational, economic, or historical context.

We have applied certain limited procedures to the required supplementary information in accordance with auditing standards generally accepted in the United States of America, which consisted of inquiries of management about the methods of preparing the information and comparing the information for consistency with management's responses to our inquiries, the basic financial statements, and other knowledge we obtained during our audits of the basic financial statements. We do not express an opinion or provide any assurance on the information because the limited procedures do not provide us with sufficient evidence to express an opinion or provide any assurance.

Our audits were conducted for the purpose of forming an opinion on the basic financial statements as a whole. The information in the *Comptrollers Viewpoint*, Sections One, Two, Three and Four of OCC's fiscal year 2012 Annual Report is presented for the purposes of additional analysis and is not a required part of the basic financial statements. Such information has not been subjected to the auditing procedures applied in the audits of the basic financial statements, and accordingly, we do not express an opinion or provide any assurance on them.

In accordance with *Government Auditing Standards,* we have also issued a report dated October 31, 2012, on our consideration of the OCC's internal control over financial reporting and a report dated October 31, 2012, on our tests of its compliance with laws, regulations, and contracts. These reports are an integral part of an audit performed in accordance with *Government Auditing Standards,* and should be read in conjunction with this report in considering the results of our audits.

GKA, P.C.

October 31, 2012

gka,p.c.
Certified Public Accountants
& Consultants

www.gkacpa.com

Independent Auditor's Report on Internal Control over Financial Reporting

Inspector General, Department of the Treasury, and
the Comptroller of the Currency:

We have audited the balance sheets and the related statements of net cost, changes in net position, and budgetary resources, hereinafter referred to as "financial statements" of the Office of the Comptroller of the Currency (OCC) as of and for the years ended September 30, 2012 and 2011, and have issued our report thereon dated October 31, 2012. We conducted our audits in accordance with auditing standards generally accepted in the United States of America; the standards applicable to financial audits contained in *Government Auditing Standards*, issued by the Comptroller General of the United States; and the applicable provisions of Office of Management and Budget (OMB) Bulletin No. 07-04, *Audit Requirements for Federal Financial Statements*, as amended.

In planning and performing our fiscal year 2012 audit, we considered the OCC's internal control over financial reporting by obtaining an understanding of the design effectiveness of OCC's internal control, determined whether these internal controls had been placed in operation, assessed control risk, and performed tests of controls as a basis for designing our auditing procedures for the purpose of expressing our opinion on the financial statements. We limited our internal control testing to those controls necessary to achieve the objectives described in OMB Bulletin No. 07-04 and *Government Auditing Standards*. We did not test all internal controls relevant to operating objectives as broadly defined by the *Federal Managers' Financial Integrity Act of 1982*, such as those controls relevant to ensuring efficient operations. The objective of our audit was not to provide an opinion on the effectiveness of OCC's internal control over financial reporting. Consequently, we do not provide an opinion on the effectiveness of OCC's internal control over financial reporting.

Our consideration of internal control over financial reporting was for the limited purpose described in the preceding paragraph and was not designed to identify all deficiencies in internal control over financial reporting that might be deficiencies, significant deficiencies, or material weaknesses. A deficiency in internal control exists when the design or operation of a control does not allow management or employees, in the normal course of performing their assigned functions, to prevent or detect and correct misstatements on a timely basis.

1015 18th Street, NW
Suite 200
Washington, DC 20036
Tel: 202-857-1777
Fax: 202-857-1778

Member of the American Institute of Certified Public Accountants

A significant deficiency is a deficiency or combination of deficiencies, in internal control that is less severe than a material weakness, yet important enough to merit attention by those charged with governance.

A material weakness is a deficiency, or a combination of deficiencies, in internal control, such that there is a reasonable possibility that a material misstatement of the entity's financial statements will not be prevented, or detected and corrected on a timely basis.

We noted certain matters discussed in Exhibit 1 involving internal control over financial reporting and its operation that we consider collectively to be a significant deficiency.

OCC management's response to the significant deficiency has not been subjected to the auditing procedures applied in the audit of the financial statements and, accordingly, we do not express an opinion or provide any form of assurance on the appropriateness of the response or the effectiveness of any corrective action described therein.

This report is intended solely for the information and use of the Management of the OCC, the Department of the Treasury Office of Inspector General, the Government Accountability Office, OMB, and the U.S. Congress, and is not intended to be, and should not be used by anyone other than these specified parties. However, this report is a matter of public record and its distribution is not limited.

GKA, P.C.

October 31, 2012

EXHIBIT 1

SIGNIFICANT DEFICIENCY

Improvements Needed in Information Technology General Controls over OCC's Financial Systems. (Repeat Condition)

During our audit, we identified certain weaknesses in OCC's IT general controls that are summarized below. Detailed findings and related recommendations will be provided to management in a separate Sensitive But Unclassified management report dated October 31, 2012.

Security Management

An entity wide information security management program is the foundation of a security control structure and a reflection of senior management's commitment to addressing security risks. As a result of our audit, we concluded that OCC Information System Security Plans (SSP) were not fully consistent with the requirements of the NIST Special Publication 800-18 Guide for Developing Security Plans for Federal Information Systems. Additionally, OCC needs to strengthen its controls over implementation of requirements pertaining to the administration of the role based security training; reviewing $MART interfaces and interconnections and ensuring that appropriate interconnection or data sharing agreements are in place.

Access Controls

Access controls should provide reasonable assurance that computer resources (data files, application programs, and computer-related facilities and equipment) are protected against unauthorized modification, disclosure, loss, or impairment. During our audit, we determined that OCC needs to strengthen its controls over implementation of requirements pertaining to password configuration settings; revoking unnecessary access accounts; completion of the exit process for terminated individuals, recordkeeping of management approval and recertification of access accounts.

Contingency Planning

Losing the capacity to process, retrieve, and protect information maintained electronically can significantly affect an agency's ability to accomplish its mission. As a result of our audit, we determined that OCC needs to strengthen its controls over the implementation of requirements pertaining to developing an executable recovery strategy, the update and maintenance of consistency between Contingency Planning documents; and periodically testing backup tapes in accordance with OCC policy.

Configuration Management

Configuration management policies, plans, and procedures should be developed, documented, and implemented at the entity wide, system, and application levels to ensure an effective configuration management process. During our audit, we determined that: OCC needs to strengthen its controls over the update of virus definitions for all relevant servers, configure information systems in accordance with documented baseline configurations, and update $MART patches and disable unnecessary services. Additionally, OCC needs to prevent developers from moving their own code into production, and ensure that operating system changes are authorized, documented and controlled through the Information Technology Services change control process.

MANAGEMENT'S RESPONSE

OCC's management concurs with the significant deficiency described in this report. Corrective actions are under way to address each recommendation, and management is confident that they will be able to rectify these deficiencies before the next *Annual Report* cycle is completed.

Independent Auditor's Report on Compliance with Laws and Regulations

The Inspector General, Department of the Treasury, and
the Comptroller of the Currency:

We have audited the balance sheets and the related statements of net cost, changes in net position, and budgetary resources, hereinafter referred to as "financial statements" of the Office of the Comptroller of the Currency (OCC) as of and for the years ended September 30, 2012 and 2011, and have issued our report thereon dated October 31, 2012. We conducted our audits in accordance with auditing standards generally accepted in the United States of America; the standards applicable to financial audits contained in *Government Auditing Standards*, issued by the Comptroller General of the United States; and, the applicable provisions of Office of Management and Budget (OMB) Bulletin No. 07-04, *Audit Requirements for Federal Financial Statements*, as amended.

The management of the OCC is responsible for complying with laws and regulations applicable to the OCC. As part of obtaining reasonable assurance about whether the OCC's financial statements are free of material misstatement, we performed tests of its compliance with certain provisions of laws and regulations and contracts, noncompliance with which could have a direct and material effect on the determination of financial statement amounts, and certain provisions of other laws and regulations specified in OMB Bulletin No. 07-04, including certain requirements referred to in Section 803(a) of the *Federal Financial Management Improvement Act (FFMIA) of 1996*. We limited our tests of compliance to the provisions described in the preceding sentence, and we did not test compliance with all laws, regulations and contracts applicable to the OCC. However, our objective was not to provide an opinion on overall compliance with laws, regulations and contracts. Accordingly, we do not express such an opinion.

The results of our tests of compliance with laws, regulations and contracts described in the preceding paragraph, exclusive of FFMIA, disclosed no instances of noncompliance or other matters that are required to be reported under *Government Auditing Standards* or OMB Bulletin No. 07-04.

Under FFMIA, we are required to report whether the OCC's financial management systems substantially comply with (1) federal financial management systems requirements, (2) applicable federal accounting standards, and (3) the United States Government Standard General Ledger at the transaction level. To meet this requirement, we performed tests of compliance with FFMIA section 803(a) requirements.

The results of our tests disclosed no instances in which the OCC's financial management systems did not substantially comply with the three requirements discussed in the preceding paragraph.

This report is intended solely for the information and use of the Management of the OCC, the Department of the Treasury Office of Inspector General, the Government Accountability Office, OMB, and U.S. Congress and is not intended to be, and should not be used by anyone other than these specified parties. However, this report is a matter of public record and its distribution is not limited.

GKA, P.C.

October 31, 2012

Performance Measures and Results

The OCC's FY 2012 performance measures, workload indicators, customer service standards, and results are presented in figure 11.

Figure 11: Performance Measures, Workload Indicators, Customer Service Standards, and Results

Strategic goal	Performance measure workload indicator customer service standard	FY 2009	FY 2010	FY 2011	FY 2012 Target	FY 2012 Actual[a]
I. A safe and sound national banking system and federal savings associations						
	Percentage of national banks and federal savings associations with composite CAMELS rating of 1 or 2[b]	82%	72%	75%	90%	*76%*
	Rehabilitated problem national banks and federal savings associations as a percentage of the problem national banks one year ago (CAMELS 3, 4, or 5)[b]	29%	22%	22%	40%	*27%*
	Percentage of national banks and federal savings associations that are well capitalized[b]	86%	91%	93%	95%	*92%*
	Percentage of critically undercapitalized banks and thrifts on which responsible action is taken within 90 calendar days after they become critically undercapitalized	100%	100%	100%	100%	100%
	Average survey response that the report of examination clearly communicated examination findings, significant issues, and the corrective actions management needed to take[c]	1.34	1.47	1.45	≤1.75	1.41
II. Fair access to financial services and fair treatment of national bank and federal savings association customers						
	Percentage of national banks and federal savings associations with consumer compliance rating of 1 or 2. For institutions with assets over $10 billion, these ratings reflect only those laws and regulations for which the OCC has enforcement and supervisory authority.	97%	96%	96%	94%	*93%*
	Percentage of community banks that are within one year of their first Intermediate Small Bank or Large Bank Community Reinvestment Act examination for which the OCC offers to provide consultation on community development opportunities	100%	100%	100%	100%	100%
	Percentage of consumer complaints closed within 60 calendar days of receipt	8%	3%	44%	80%	56%
	Number of consumer complaints opened/closed or referred during the fiscal year[d]	58,810/ 32,533	80,336/ 79,660	85,127/ 85,128	72,000/ 70,000	66,161/ 59,130
III. A flexible legal and regulatory framework that enables national banks and federal savings associations to provide a full, competitive array of financial services consistent with statutory and prudential safety and soundness constraints						
	Percentage of external legal opinions issued within established time frames	88%	85%	91%	86%	90%
	Number of external legal opinions issued during the fiscal year	53	64	77	60	59
	Percentage of licensing applications and notices filed electronically	51%	44%	53%	35%	42%
	Number of licensing applications and notices filed electronically during the fiscal year	1,681	1,440	1,610	1,200	1,374
	Percentage of licensing applications and notices completed within established time frames	95%	96%	97%	95%	98%
	Number of licensing applications and notices completed during the fiscal year	1,471	1,344	1,382	1,700	1,614
	Average survey rating of the overall licensing services provided by the OCC[e]	1.25	1.15	1.31	≤1.5	1.22
IV. A competent, highly motivated, and diverse workforce that makes effective use of OCC resources						
	Total OCC costs relative to every $100,000 in assets regulated	$8.81	$9.28	$8.76	$9.22	*$10.51*

Note: Before FY 2012, OCC performance measures included only supervision of national banks. On July 21, 2011, the OCC assumed responsibility for regulating federal savings associations. Therefore, FY 2012 is the new baseline year for the OCC, with new measures that include both national banks and federal savings associations. All data before FY 2012 include only national banks.

[a] The FY 2012 performance numbers shown in bold italics are estimates. Some performance data are obtained from quarterly call reports from banks. The September 30, 2012, call reports are not due until 30 or 45 days after the end of the period. Additionally, examinations concluded late in the fiscal year are not finalized for another 30 to 60 days. As a result, complete fiscal year data are not yet available; therefore, estimates have been reported.

[b] These performance measures for FY 2012 are below target primarily because of the difficult economic situation the entire financial industry is facing. The OCC continues to closely monitor the capital levels and performance of all its banks and, when necessary, initiates formal and informal agreements to enhance its level of supervision.

[c] The examination survey is based on a five-point scale, in which 1 indicates complete agreement and 5 indicates complete disagreement.

[d] The total complaint numbers include referrals to the Federal Reserve Board, the FDIC, the National Credit Union Administration, or any other agency or entity that is not a national bank, as well as those complaints serviced on behalf of the CFPB.

[e] The licensing survey is based on a five-point scale, in which 1 indicates outstanding and 5 indicates significantly deficient.

Improper Payments Elimination and Recovery Act

The Improper Payments Elimination and Recovery Act of 2012, as implemented by the OMB, requires federal agencies to review all programs and activities annually and identify those that may be susceptible to significant erroneous payments. The OCC analyzed payments (excluding payroll) made during FY 2012 and identified 11 erroneous payments requiring adjustments totaling $573. Erroneous payments are identified and monitored daily to ensure prompt recovery. The underlying causes and contributing factors are identified quickly, and control measures are implemented to prevent additional erroneous payments.

The OCC corrected and recovered all erroneous payments made during the year. Figure 12 summarizes the OCC's erroneous payments for FY 2012 and FY 2011.

Figure 12: Erroneous Payments

	FY 2012	FY 2011
Number of payments	11	52
Dollar value of adjustments	$573	$17,060

Source: OCC data.

Assurance Statement

The Office of the Comptroller of the Currency (OCC) met the internal control requirements of the Federal Managers' Financial Integrity Act (FMFIA), the Federal Financial Management Improvement Act (FFMIA), and Office of Management and Budget (OMB) Circular A-123 during fiscal year (FY) 2012.

The OCC's systems of management control ensure that

a) programs achieve their intended results;
b) resources are used in accordance with the agency's mission;
c) programs and resources are protected from waste, fraud, and mismanagement;
d) laws and regulations are followed;
e) controls are sufficient to minimize improper or erroneous payments;
f) performance information is reliable;
g) system security is in substantial compliance with relevant requirements;
h) continuity of operations planning in critical areas is sufficient to reduce risk to reasonable levels; and
i) financial management systems are in compliance with federal financial systems standards, i.e., FMFIA Section 4 and FFMIA.

I am providing unqualified assurance that the above listed management control objectives were achieved by the OCC without material weakness during FY 2012. Specifically, this assurance is provided relative to Sections 2 and 4 of the FMFIA.

The OCC conducted its assessment of the effectiveness of its internal control over financial reporting, which includes the safeguarding of assets and compliance with applicable laws and regulations, in accordance with the requirements of Appendix A of OMB Circular A-123. Based on the results of this evaluation, the OCC can provide unqualified assurance that its internal control over financial reporting was operating effectively as of June 30, 2012, and no material weaknesses were found in the design or operation of the internal control over financial reporting.

I am reporting substantial compliance with the requirements imposed by the FFMIA. The agency's internal assessment and the external auditors' report on internal control identified a significant control deficiency related to information technology general controls in the areas of security management, access controls, contingency planning, and configuration management. A plan of corrective action is in place to address these issues during FY 2013.

I am also providing unqualified assurance that our supervision programs achieved intended results despite the extraordinary challenges that continued to confront national banks and federal savings associations (collectively, banks).

Operating environments for the OCC and the banking industry remain challenging. While domestic conditions are improved overall, U.S. banks with Eurozone banking operations confront significant risks associated with potential sovereign defaults or countries' exit from the Eurozone. Nevertheless, on average, balance sheets are stronger, earnings are improving, and the number of problem institutions and institutional failures, while still too high, is declining.

The industry continues to recover from the credit and capital market challenges of the financial crisis. At the same time, however, operational risk, generally defined as the risk of loss due to failures of people, processes, systems, and external events, is increasing. Such risk is heightened when these systems and procedures are most complex.

The OCC is responding to these challenges with enhanced supervision, effective policy development, rulemaking, risk monitoring, and examination support. Through joint efforts with other federal banking agencies, the OCC also continues to implement provisions of the Dodd–Frank Act. While minimizing regulatory burden, managing the complexity of and interaction between Dodd–Frank and other statutory and regulatory provisions will continue to require extensive interagency consultation and coordination.

This fiscal year, the OCC completed the integration of 668 Office of Thrift Supervision (OTS) employees, successfully moving to one regulator with one mission to supervise national banks and federal savings associations. Continued progress in integrating OTS and OCC policy and examination platforms remains a top priority. Early in 2013, the OCC will launch an aggressive cross-credentialing program to enable examiners to become certified to lead examinations of both national banks and federal savings associations. Our goal is to have many examiners cross-credentialed for maximum resource efficiency and flexibility.

Other important initiatives include extensive examiner assignment rotations, extensive examiner training in risk specialties under the tutelage of experienced team leaders, and the recruitment of individuals with industry or examination experience in specialty areas such as commercial and retail credit, operational risk, Bank Secrecy Act/Anti-Money Laundering (BSA/AML), and consumer compliance.

We are also devoting considerable resources to developing or improving risk assessment and monitoring analytical tools, including an internal radar risk rating and ranking process for the banking system; a customized package of early warning indicators to detect risks and trends building in the system; and enhanced periodic reports to identify and monitor risks. The OCC's National Risk Committee has begun publishing a *Semiannual Risk Perspective* report to give bankers, examiners, and the public the OCC perspective on key risks and issues facing national banks and federal savings institutions. The first public version of this report was issued in July 2012. In the Eurozone area, added risks include the disruption of financial market infrastructure, the potential devolution of the Euro and introduction of new currencies, the redenomination of financial instruments, and the introduction of capital and exchange controls by a country that exits the Eurozone. In our supervisory role, we are evaluating the range of exposures our institutions could face from direct investment, contagion, and operating risks and actions taken to mitigate or contain those risks. This evaluation involves reviewing banks' contingency plans; monitoring progress through regular meetings with bank and thrift management; and ensuring that capital, reserves, and liquidity are strong and resilient.

The OCC communicated its elevated expectations for corporate governance and oversight to the large banks under its supervision. We are also measuring progress in achieving: board of directors' willingness to provide credible challenge; talent management

and compensation; defining and communicating risk appetite across the company; development and maintenance of strong audit and risk management functions; and sanctity of the national bank and federal savings association charters.

The OCC continues to be represented in various interagency and international groups, including the Federal Financial Institutions Examination Council, the Financial Stability Oversight Council, the Basel Committee on Banking Supervision, and the Financial Stability Board.

In addition, the OCC continues to work closely with an interagency group to develop comprehensive and consistently applied and enforced national foreclosure servicing standards. We are ensuring that the largest regulated mortgage servicers under our consent orders correct identified deficiencies, and we remain committed to transparency in this process. We released an updated "Interim Status Report" and joined with other regulators to release the "Interagency Guidance on Mortgage Servicing Practices Concerning Military Homeowners With Permanent Change of Station Orders." We also published a foreclosure management bulletin to alert large banks to oversight and management expectations, and we are examining for compliance.

To reaffirm the importance of strong risk management, we issued guidance to bankers including an updated concentrations handbook, a capital planning bulletin, a statement on accounting and reporting troubled debt restructurings, and interagency guidance on stress testing for banks with more than $10 billion in consolidated assets as a means to better understand the range of a banking organization's potential risk exposures. To clarify expectations for community banks, we issued separate guidance on the use of stress testing in community banks. While we expect community banks to identify and assess key vulnerabilities and incorporate those assessments into their risk management, business strategies, and capital planning processes, the guidance emphasizes that there is a range of fairly simple tools they can use for such analyses. Concurrent with that guidance, we also made available to national banks and federal savings associations a stress-testing tool to assess key vulnerabilities in community banks' income-producing commercial real estate portfolios.

In addition to rulemaking, bulletins, and other guidance, the OCC is investing significant resources to conduct outreach programs on national, regional, and local levels. During the year, the OCC hosted banking outreach sessions throughout the country for bankers and bank directors to provide updates and educational materials on current issues and supervisory expectations. In addition to these face-to-face meetings, we conducted several teleconferences on supervisory topics, including small business lending. We also hosted a series of annual workshops for bank and thrift directors, a program that is a direct outgrowth of interaction with the industry.

We have increased our staffing levels at the large banks we supervise, improving communication while aiding prompt monitoring and assessment.

Members of our nation's armed forces and their families sacrifice much to safeguard the liberties we enjoy. Because of the extraordinary hardships of military service, the law provides certain protections to our servicemembers. In FY 2012, the OCC and the U.S. Department of Justice have helped ensure that servicemembers received every benefit they were entitled to under the law, and we are directing national banks and federal savings associations to correct any found violations of the Servicemembers Civil Relief Act (SCRA). We are also revising and strengthening our examination policies for SCRA compliance.

Another area of the agency's focus is BSA/AML compliance, and we have implemented new approaches to BSA/AML to ensure that deficiencies are considered in a safety and soundness context. The OCC is committed to ensuring that the institutions under its supervision have effective controls in place to safeguard them from being used as vehicles to launder money for drug traffickers and transnational and other criminal organizations, or to facilitate the financing of terrorist acts.

The OCC recognizes that it must be vigilant against the determination and ingenuity of those who commit financial crimes. We also recognize that technical innovations, new and more convenient financial

services products, and globalization trends are rapidly changing the BSA/AML landscape. These are major challenges for both the financial services industry and its regulators, and we are committed to meeting those challenges.

The OCC also continues to address its disaster recovery capability with a comprehensive phased plan for the next three years to meet the organization's information technology needs. Phase one is underway, with the OCC moving to a new, state-of-the-art, highly secure, and fully redundant data center. Phase two is also underway, with the OCC's critical e-mail infrastructure, including BlackBerry servers, already hosted at a fully redundant data center in Charleston, W. Va. By June 30, 2014, I anticipate receiving a proposal for phase three, the OCC's new disaster recovery strategy and roadmap.

Analytical Basis of Assurance Statement

The OCC evaluated its management controls in accordance with the FY 2012 Secretary's Assurance Statement Guidance of June 22, 2012, and considered the following guidance:

- OMB Circular A-127, Financial Management Systems;
- OMB Circular A-130 Revised, Management of Federal Information Resources;
- OMB Circular A-11, Preparation, Submission, and Execution of the Budget;
- OMB Bulletin 06-03, Audit Requirements for Federal Financial Statements;
- Statement on Auditing Standards No. 115, Communicating Internal Control Related Matters Identified in an Audit; and
- Treasury Directive 40-04, Treasury Internal (Management) Control Program.

Information considered in our control assessment included the following:

- FMFIA certifications submitted by each Executive Committee member;
- FFMIA certification submitted by our Chief Financial Officer;
- The OCC's Strategic Risk Management Plan;
- Results of internal control testing under OMB Circular A-123, Appendix A;

- Executive Committee descriptions of business unit quality management programs;
- Results of control self-assessments completed by OCC managers in FY 2012;
- Audit reports and evaluations issued by the Government Accountability Office (GAO) and the Office of the Inspector General;
- Results of other external and internal reviews;
- Assessment of the Improper Payments Elimination and Recovery Act submitted to the U.S. Department of the Treasury in FY 2012;
- GAO Core Financial System Requirements Checklist;
- FFMIA Risk Model and Financial Management System Self-Assessment Checklists submitted to the Treasury Department in July 2012;
- Unqualified and timely audit opinion on FY 2011 financial statements; and
- Certified public accountant Gardiner, Kamya and Associates' October 11, 2012 status report on the FY 2012 financial statement audit.

Thomas J. Curry
Comptroller of the Currency

Abbreviations

ASC	Accounting Standards Codification
BSA/AML	Bank Secrecy Act and Anti-Money Laundering
CAMELS	capital, asset quality, management, earnings, liquidity, and sensitivity to market risk
CFPB	Consumer Financial Protection Bureau
CMP	civil money penalty
CRA	Community Reinvestment Act
CSRS	Civil Service Retirement System
FAQ	Frequently Asked Questions
FASAB	Federal Accounting Standards Advisory Board
FASB	Financial Accounting Standards Board
FBWT	fund balance with Treasury
FDIC	Federal Deposit Insurance Corporation
FEGLI	Federal Employees' Group Life Insurance
FEHB	Federal Employees Health Benefits
FERS	Federal Employees Retirement System
FFMIA	Federal Financial Management Improvement Act
FMFIA	Federal Managers' Financial Integrity Act
FY	fiscal year
GAAP	generally accepted accounting principles
GAO	Government Accountability Office
IRR	interest rate risk
JPMC	JP Morgan Chase
LSS	Lean Six Sigma

NPR	notice of proposed rulemaking
NRC	National Risk Committee
OCC	Office of the Comptroller of the Currency
OM	Office of Management
OMB	Office of Management and Budget
OMWI	Office of Minority and Women Inclusion
OPM	Office of Personnel Management
OTS	Office of Thrift Supervision
PSH	permanent supportive housing
SCRA	Servicemembers Civil Relief Act
SFFAS	Statement of Federal Financial Accounting Standards
USC	U.S. Code

Index

O

W

Walsh, John
    Acting Comptroller, 27
    Dodd–Frank implications, 19
    OCC and OTS integration, 23
    Volcker rule, 22
Wells Fargo, 18
Williams, Julie L., 28, 29
women-owned businesses, 23

Y

Year in Review, 7–24

In "The Abraham Lincoln Mural (Conferring With Salmon P. Chase)" (1922), the artist N.C. Wyeth depicted the two men working on national banking legislation.

Courtesy of Langham Hotel, Boston, Mass.

www.ingramcontent.com/pod-product-compliance
Lightning Source LLC
Chambersburg PA
CBHW080318290526
45790CB00005B/2093